INDIA
BELOVED OF HEAVEN

INDIA
BELOVED OF HEAVEN

BRENTON THOBURN BADLEY AND W. F. OLDHAM

GYAN

Published by

Gyan Publishing House
5, Ansari Road
Daryaganj, New Delhi-110002
Phone: 011-47034999, 9811692060
E-mail: books@gyanbooks.com

Distribution Network
gyanbooks.com
India, USA, Canada, UK, Australia

ISBN: 978-93-7014-043-1 (PB)

First Published, 1918

2nd Impression 2025

Printed at: Gyan Press, Delhi.

INDIA BELOVED OF HEAVEN
Arthur BRENTON THOBURN BADLEY AND W. F. OLDHAM

INDIA
BELOVED OF HEAVEN

BY

BRENTON THOBURN BADLEY

IN COLLABORATION WITH

OSCAR MacMILLAN BUCK

JAMES JAY KINGHAM

WITH AN INTRODUCTION BY

BISHOP W. F. OLDHAM

CONTENTS

ILLUSTRATIONS

PREFACE

THIS is not a book of fiction, though there are elements of fiction in some of the chapters. The chapters by Mr. Kingham are faithful records of what he himself has experienced in India. The stories by the two other writers are founded on fact, though in the matter of detail and treatment the prerogatives of the story-writer have been assumed.

The stories in these pages give some idea of the far-reaching changes in life and thought that are so rapidly coming over India. They have been written by three Lovers of Hindustan, seeking to bring America and India still closer together in the bonds of the most disinterested international friendship our world has yet known.

The unusually fine illustrations by Mr. Jack Flanagan, of New York, have been added through the generosity of friends of the author without cost to the publishers.

B. T. B.

INTRODUCTION

THE old India passes. The dreamy, puzzling, lovable, lotus-eating land, with her beauty and tenderness, yet hiding much that hurts her children, is rapidly undergoing a new birth.

Not only do her forms change; her brooding spirit within and all her outlook change —and yet her winsomeness remains. It increases.

The poison flowers wither, but the champadas and the jasmines bloom. Languorous odors fill the air, and the bulbul and the nightingales sing; but the hiss of the cobra dies down.

The healing Christ is somewhere around. His transforming touch is on India.

This sweet, strange land, with her baffling life, can be interpreted only by her lovers. The writers of these tales are such—two of them she bore on her bosom from helpless babyhood. All three have drunk of Ganga's water and have cried "Bande Mataram"—"Hail, blessed mother!"

Who would learn a little more of India, the beloved of heaven, let him read.

W. F. OLDHAM.

I

ON HIS MAJESTY'S SERVICE

IT was Gulab Singh's luck to run right into a good thing quite unexpectedly. He was in Bombay, on a trip from the docks to the hotel, having failed to get in touch with any prospective patrons among the several who had landed that day. He saw a *sahib* leaning out over a pile of luggage, shouting at the driver of the victoria. Just as the carriage came up to him a gust of wind blew the gentleman's *sola topi* off his head. Gulab Singh ran and picked it up, brushing it with his *jharan* as he handed it to the irate gentleman.

"Look here," exclaimed the handsome young *sahib,* "can you tell this blooming idiot to drive me to the Army and Navy Co-operative Stores?"

Now, Gulab Singh had picked up a little English, and the Army and Navy Stores he knew anyway. Accordingly, he jumped up on the coachman's box and enlightened the driver, who happened to be a greenhorn, supplying for his brother for a day.

Gulab Singh was an up-country man, who had failed to secure service and was now in Bombay. He had had to borrow money to make the journey, for even the third-class ticket from Agra had cost him more than he could hope to earn in a month. He had been spending his time partly at the docks where the P. & O. liners come in, and partly at the Taj Mahal and other hotels, hoping that some young English officer just arrived from England, might take him on as "bearer" or valet.

Not that Gulab Singh—which, being interpreted, means "Rose Lion"—had had much experience. He had served a young lieutenant at Meerut for a few months, and at Agra had had a few transient *naukaris*—services. He was young, only twenty-four. His chief dependence was on some letters of recommendation—"chits" we call them in India—that he could borrow from an uncle who bore the same name and who had served many families, chiefly military, in Bombay.

Gulab Singh meets the Captán Sahib

A few of the best and most recent of these he now had in his possession for possible use!

After the sahib had bought what he needed at the Army and Navy Stores, he noticed that the extra man continued on the box with the driver to the hotel. When his luggage had all been placed on the veranda there, he was faced by the salaaming Gulab Singh, who, with "chits" in hand, offered his willing services to the *huzúr,* "the Presence."

"Huzúr is going up-country and will need a servant?"

"Yes, but I'm blowed if I know how you found it out!"

Gulab Singh was not the only Indian with a ready imagination and ability to make a shrewd guess!

By this time several of the "chits" had been opened up, ready for inspection. The young captain, for such he was, took one and read:

"Gulab Singh, bearer, has served me for several months. He knows how to take care of an officer's sword and uniform, and I found him very handy about the Mess and Polo grounds. He seems to have a knack of doing very well a variety of things that are a help to a military officer in this beastly land. He leaves my service as I have been posted to the hills and he prefers to remain on the plains."

This was signed by a lieutenant of the "Fourth Ghurka Rifles." It sufficed our young captain, who pushed aside the rest of the letters, including most valuable ones that belonged to the elder Gulab Singh.

"I don't go much on letters. I'm willing to try you. Take charge of these things. Put those two bags," tapping them with his cane, "into my room here, and see that the rest of the stuff gets to the 'Victoria Terminus' for the Punjab mail this evening. I'm off to Meerut."

And so Gulab Singh was again an *afsar's naukar*—an officer's servant. Between twelve and two o'clock he made a hasty trip to his uncle's to return the borrowed letters.

"Rám's name be praised!" he exclaimed, "a young captán *sahib* has taken me on. We leave for Meerut this evening. Here are your letters."

Saying this, he produced all the letters,

including several contained in a cloth-lined envelope, with "On His Majesty's Service" printed across the top left-hand corner. It was a stout covering, and showed long and hard usage. He had doubtless picked it up somewhere.

"You still carry those old letters of your father's that he got from the colonel *sahib.*"

"Yes," replied Gulab Singh. "Since my father died, I keep them with me when I am gone from home. Who knows when the old chappar (thatch) that covers us may not catch fire and burn up everything?"

He handled the envelope with reverence, and added: "It has also a letter that was given by the *sahib* whose life my grandfather saved in the time of the great *gadr* [the Indian Mutiny of 1857]. My father often told me to take special care of that."

Sentiment plays a great part in the lives of India's sons.

Now, it is not the object of this story to follow the brief career of Captain Clyde Boynton Stanhope in India. He had landed at Bombay in 1912, and in 1914 the great war broke out. That changed the career of hundreds of officers in the British army in India. He had come to love India, and though he had never been there before, he could not forget that both his father and grandfather, the one in civil, the other in military service, had given their best years to this land.

His first days in Meerut were lived as in a dream. How strange that he should be in this Indian city, where fifty-five years before his grandfather had been among the few who escaped in the sudden massacre that ushered in the tragic rebellion of the sepoys! He visited the scenes of the massacre, and tried to imagine that hot and bloody Sunday of May, 1857, when the houses of the European residents had been set on fire, and men, women, and children had been butchered as they fled from the flaming, thatch-roofed bungalows.

The soldiers were at church—the parade service—and were there without their rifles! They had been set upon in the midst of the service. Never since that day have British soldiers attended a parade service without their rifles and bayonets.

Yet Meerut was quiet and beautiful now. What superb avenues of shady *shisham* trees! What fine polo and parade grounds! What pride and interest the officers took in their men—descendants of those who had shared in the massacre of the earlier day.

When the call came to England and France, Captain Stanhope's regiment was among the first to embark. He was again at Bombay. Again his luggage was on the veranda of the Taj Mahal hotel—but considerably less in amount. Gulab Singh was also there. The English officer had come to have a real regard for his "bearer." The young servant combined devotion and dignity in his service, and with many shortcomings—among which lying figured duly—still showed an undoubted and unusual attachment to his young master. He served with growing admiration the fine, strong, enthusiastic young officer. The fact was that the open, generous nature of his *sahib* had won his heart.

When it came to the question of his master's departure for Walayat (England), Gulab Singh steadily maintained that he would go along. As a first step, he came on to Bombay, and now he insisted that he should cross the seas. Was the *sahib* not *able* to arrange it?

"O, yes, that part of it is all right, Gulab Singh, for the colonel has permitted officers to take their servants as far as London, if they choose. But what will you *do* when you get there?"

"Do, Sahib? Is the great *larai* [battle] not on? Are you not going to fight? Can I not be with you on the campaign there, as on the military excursions here?"

Now, Gulab Singh had no idea of what he talked about. He was imagining a whole lot, and had nothing to draw on except his limited Indian experience. The fact is, he longed to go. To him it seemed now like a question of personal loyalty to his *sahib*.

"Namak—halál" was the greatest word in the vocabulary of Gulab Singh. Literally it means "loyalty to one's salt."

"I have eaten the *Sarcar's* [government's] salt," said he. "I think I can help you there. Do not refuse me permission, Sahib!"

And so Gulab Singh crossed the great *kálá páni,* the "black water"—ocean. Thousands and multiplied thousands of India's sons were soon to do the same. A new day had come for India. Indian troops were to go to Europe. They had fought under British leadership in Africa, Egypt, China—but who had expected to live to see this great new day? A mighty thrill swept through her ancient peoples. New dignity entered into their life; a new future began to open to their enlarged vision. India would never be the same again!

For Gulab Singh, the new exalted life had already begun. His wonder daily increased. The nearer he got to England the higher rose his pride. He was, at last, at a man's work! There was something else—he did not know it, but it was there nevertheless. The Aryan blood in him was astir.

We do well to think of this—the meeting in India, after thousands of years of separation, of the two branches of the great Aryan family. The gulf that has separated them has changed both from the type in the original family home in Western Asia, but there they stand at last again, brethren, side by side! Save for color, and certain admixtures of other blood, the two are still much alike. The clear-cut features remain the same, the same fine sensitive nature marks the two. The Englishman or the American, when face to face with either Chinese, Japanese, or African, cannot but feel that he sees a man radically different from himself. When he meets the Indian it is different—there is an instinctive resumption of the fellowship broken off in the dim past.

Neither Gulab Singh nor Captain Stanhope thought of these things, but it was interesting to note the growing regard of the *sahib* for his servant, and the increasing respect of the valet for his master. And so the voyage terminated. While the young Captain spent a brief period of leave with his people, Gulab Singh, as a matter of course, stayed on to serve him. When the young officer was ordered to camp, there still was no reason why his Indian servant should be separated from him. But when, a few weeks later, the regiment was ordered off to France, there was a real question to be settled.

Again Gulab Singh prevailed. He had come thus far—what was there now to do except to go on? Surely, if the *sahib* had need of him in England, he could make some use of him in France. Were the two countries, then, so utterly different?

Thus we find Gulab Singh at last on French soil, behind the British fighting lines. Many were the ways in which he made himself useful to his young *captán sahib* during those strenuous and perilous days. Often did Captain Stanhope bless the day when he picked up the faithful Gulab Singh in the streets of Bombay. Had not his first, unasked, service of help been prophetic of all the assistance he had been rendering since?

After several weeks, during which Gulab Singh went through years of experience, there came a terrible day—one of those days that will go down in history. Gulab Singh and his beloved captain were in the retreat from Mons. Now, Gulab Singh did not know why a British army should have to retreat. He had not been brought up on that kind of tradition! He had yet to learn the glory of that wondrous feat of courage and endurance, whereby so slender an army was able to foil the purposes of the Prussian hordes, even in the act of falling back before the terrible onrush of their overwhelming numbers.

There came a perilous day toward the end of that almost impossible feat of arms by England, France, and Canada, when Gulab Singh's master had to hold a position with his company, covering the retreat of important detachments. It was evident to any man that it was a time to earn glory, but not to save life. The young captain explained the situation to his faithful Indian servant, and told him to fall back. Gulab Singh remonstrated.

"If there is danger for my Sahib, he will need me all the more," said he.

"It is not a question of danger merely, Gulab Singh," exclaimed the Captain, "it is a matter of death."

"If death is preferred by my Sahib, it is good enough for me," he said, earnestly, and refused to take the vanishing opportunity to withdraw.

We shall not be able to follow the fortunes of the fighting there during those fateful hours. The undying heroism of those who died in khaki that day may never be chronicled.

Captain Stanhope's company held their ground till the end, and saved the situation at that point. Only a few wounded men came out of that conflict to tell how the foe had been checked.

The last to fall was the captain himself. Gulab Singh, who had been in the thick of it all, came instantly to his side. He was only wounded.

"Go back, Gulab Singh. There is still time. Tell the Colonel Sahib that we did not yield."

Gulab Singh did not heed—he was concerned only over the stream of blood that flowed from the captain's wound. He bound it up as best he could, tearing long strips from his turban to do so. Then he said—

"Come, Sahib, I will help you back."

There was nothing to be done by remaining. The khaki forms on the ground moved not.

Slowly and painfully the two made their way back, Gulab Singh skillfully taking advantage of every bit of cover, and sometimes almost carrying his master.

It must have been a stirring sight—the Aryan brown and the Aryan white, on the battlefields of France! Typical too of India helping England in her hour of need. And Gulab Singh was only in the vanguard of the one million sons of India who were shortly to respond to the call of the empire, for the cause of justice, liberty, democracy. And Gulab Singh was typical in this, also, that he came as a volunteer. There has been no conscription in India; no draft is needed to bring her millions on to the scene of freedom's war against tyranny!

The dangerous strip of land had just been safely covered by the wounded, now almost fainting officer, and his faithful Indian servant. They had just got touch with a British column.

"You are safe, Sahib!" exclaimed the

"The Aryan white and the Aryan brown, on the battlefields of France"

proud and happy Gulab Singh, as he caught sight of British uniforms near, and saw some soldiers advance to their help.

The captain lost consciousness and Gulab Singh allowed his form to sink upon the ground. He kneeled beside him to adjust the bandages and stanch the flow of blood. They were still exposed to danger from an occasional enemy bullet.

"Hé, Parmeshwar," he exclaimed, "grant that he may live!"

The men coming forward to aid the officer had seen Gulab Singh kneel to help the wounded officer. The next instant they saw him fall forward on his face.

He did not move. Gulab Singh was dead!

The party coming up found that the Indian had been shot in the breast and killed instantly. The officer was still alive.

They carried them both to the rear of the lines.

The captain regained consciousness, but was delirious.

"Go back, Gulab Singh. . . . Bring the tea and toast. . . . I'm going to the Polo ground. . . . See, there's the *paltan* [regiment]. . . . Steady, boys—we can hold them!"

He was taken to the base hospital, where, with careful nursing, he recovered.

When he was able to understand things, he was told of the death of his Indian servant. They did not need to add that Gulab Singh had saved his life. He knew that.

Among the things found on Gulab Singh's body was an envelope. It contained a letter, said the nurse, signed by Colonel James Randolph Stanhope, and so it had been saved for Captain Stanhope.

"Perhaps it was an ancestor of yours in the British army of India?" asked the nurse.

"It is my grandfather's name. Let me see the letter."

A soiled, much worn, cloth-lined envelope was handed to him.

The first thing he noticed was that the top left-hand corner bore the familiar words in print—"On His Majesty's Service."

Carefully the young captain took out a faded, much-creased letter. He glanced first at the signature. It was that of his own grandfather, colonel of the 9th Sikh Cavalry. The date was October 30th, 1858. He read:

"On leaving India I take keen pleasure in writing this letter for Gulab Singh. For seven years he served me faithfully as bearer. His work was always satisfactory —a service that he crowned by helping me to escape death at the hands of the mutineers in Meerut. Had it not been for his timely and unhesitating assistance, both Mrs. Stanhope and myself must certainly have met a cruel death at the hands of the rebellious sepoys.

"I have made suitable provision for him and his family and am both proud and grateful to accede to his request for a personal letter. The Stanhopes must ever remain grateful to the house of Gulab Singh."

The captain lay motionless a long time, holding the letter in his hand. The thing was fairly overpowering. Gulab Singh's grandfather had saved his grandfather's life! And here he himself was lying safe in a base hospital, saved by the devotion of the grandson!

"Grateful to the house of Gulab Singh!" And he could not express his gratitude to his own Gulab Singh!

Then he read the letter once more. After that he folded it up and put it back in the old, cloth-lined envelope. This time he noticed that a hole had been torn in the top left-hand corner of the envelope, almost obliterating the word "His."

He turned the envelope over. It was stained with blood. The hole was made by the bullet that killed Gulab Singh!

His eyes took on a far-off look. His thoughts went back to Meerut—to the bloodstained Meerut of 1857—to the quiet and beautiful Meerut of 1914.

If he lived through the war, he would return to India, look up the family of Gulab Singh and honor and reward them.

The Stanhopes were still more indebted to "the house of Gulab Singh."

His gaze rested again on the envelope. He read, "On His Majesty's Service."

"Ay, Gulab Singh," he said aloud, "both you and I, both England and India, to the glorious end—'On His Majesty's Service!' "

II

PONNIAH

IN the classroom of the old Jesuit mission at Tuticorin a boy of sixteen was mulling over his lessons, humming them aloud, and sometimes singing them in competition with the twenty-five others of his class whose nasal voices blended and discorded with his from time to time. His blue-black hair was luxuriant and gathered in a knot at the back of his shapely head, but tendrils escaped about the finely modeled forehead and he brushed them back from his brows without a moment's cessation of his reading, in his carefully modulated, expressive sing-song.

Their Tamil lesson finished, at the teacher's word the pupils gathered up their books and placed them in small book-sacks, which they rolled up and tied to carry home. Ponniah remained to question his teacher, a Tamil man of the same caste as himself, presenting certain physical resemblances, though somewhat heavier and taller than the slim brown youth who stood before him.

"Sir, this lesson was most delightful, and I have been waiting to ask you a question on its application. Here is a line in the stanza, about which Kasthuri and I argued. He said it was wrong, but I held it is right, and said I should ask you."

"Ponniah, there are some very remarkable expressions in the stanza, but the grammar is correct. Where did you find it?"

"Teacher, I am fascinated by the classic writers, and imitating their style, I wrote it myself."

"This is not bad for a boy. Let me have it to-night and you may get it in the morning."

So, the teacher took the roll of manuscript covered with Ponniah's somewhat irregular penmanship, and Ponniah with a low bow and the most respectful salaam passed out of the room into the open sunlight. As he stepped outside the building he walked almost into the arms of his uncle, who was waiting for him. Not taking time to let

Ponniah get his breath, the older man began speaking.

"Ponniah," he said, "everything is ready for your wedding to my daughter Pushpam. The guests are come, the wedding supper is cooking, the gifts are ready, the Brahmans wait, only the bridegroom is lacking. Come, enter my oxcart; let us get home to our village."

"But, uncle, I have told you again and again that I should not marry till I had completed my education. How can I study and succeed after taking a wife? If I spend much time on my books she will be jealous."

"Ponniah, who are you to argue with me? Your people and mine have arranged all things. You have but to obey. Come with me at once!"

But Ponniah merely looked a moment into the darkening face of his uncle, and then turned to run swiftly away. At the exit from the great stone-walled compound which contained the Jesuit mission buildings, he turned his head to see if he had gained upon his pursuing uncle, and at the same moment two heavy hands fell upon his slim figure and he was thrown to the ground by a man who had stood concealed by the great gateway. A moment later his uncle too was upon him and the two raised him to his feet. The struggle was in vain, so he allowed them to lead him to an oxcart standing in the street near by. They loaded him inside its capacious ribs and the uncle ascended behind him, while the opportune ally seized a goad and drove the oxen more rapidly than such great beasts generally travel, out through the narrow streets and at last into the open country. Then on and on till the stars shone out and the youthful prisoner was sound asleep in the bumping cart, between his two captors.

They reached their destination before midnight, a large prosperous village with towering palm trees and drooping plantains, great fields of grain waving under the moonlight which lighted the broad plains and even showed the far-off mountains. As they dismounted in the courtyard of a great brick dwelling they found the wedding guests asleep on mats and cots which filled and overflowed the surrounding sheds.

Their showy garments and the filmy white cloths spread over their heads gave them a mysterious appearance, but it was only a few minutes till the driver had unhitched his oxen, placed fodder before them in their stalls, and taken his place among the silent forms, while Ponniah's uncle merely relaxed beside the silent form he was watching.

A little later he had fallen sound asleep and there was not a sound in the courtyard, except some snoring among the wedding guests and the cattle munching their fodder.

A mosquito lighting upon Ponniah's uncovered face awakened him, and he gazed about him. Everyone was asleep and he had no difficulty slipping out of the wagon without arousing his uncle. From the great open courtyard he passed into the house, which was even more completely full of people than the courtyard, but here were only women, women sleeping as soundly as the men outside. Ponniah looked about inside the building for a place of concealment. At first he thought there was none, but he remembered a great grain jar which reached nearly to the ceiling and was some eight feet in diameter. In the darkness he groped carefully till he found it, then, avoiding one of the sleepers whose shimmering white garments warned him of her presence, he climbed from a wooden mortar up to its rim and threw himself over the rim and inside the jar. It was half full of rice and he was soon sound asleep in that warm chamber.

When he awoke the whole house was in an uproar. Every one asked his neighbor, "Where is Ponniah?" They searched high and low for him, dragged the wells and cisterns, hunted in the woods, searched the neighboring houses, but Ponniah was not to be found. Secure in his hiding place, he listened to the comments and bewildered questions of the guests and of his own family. The day passed, but Hindu weddings are not a matter of a day, they require three days, and on the third day, because much treasure had been spent and because a bride whose wedding is postponed can never be married, they married his uncle's daughter to another cousin, one less fortunately endowed than Ponniah both by nature and by inheritance from his parents.

On the third day the wedding was over and the guests were feasted and bade farewell to the parents of the bride and the bridegroom. Ponniah, though within sound of the feasting, had had no part in it and was stiff with enforced movelessness and hungry with long fasting. When certain that all had left the room, he stood up and looked over the rim of the great jar. Something of the feast remained. He could eat and hide till evening, then steal away in the darkness. He climbed over the rim and lowered himself to the floor, dropping stiffly the last two feet of the distance, and almost at the same moment the door opened and his uncle entered.

"Ha!" he shouted. "Now I have you who caused me to marry my daughter to a poor man, you who escaped and deceived me. You will pay the penalty now. Scoundrel!"

And he seized Ponniah and tied him to a pillar that supported the roof, while he went out to look for a rod with which to beat him. While he was gone his nephew slipped his slim wrists out of the tight lashing, then placed them so that his uncle would not suspect him, remaining in the same posture with his arms raised and encircling the pillar.

The rod was a stout bamboo, and it whistled through the air as his uncle put his force into every blow. Ponniah could only bear two or three. He turned suddenly and, to his uncle's great surprise, seized the bamboo club and struck his assailant, almost stunning him. He then rushed from the house as fast as his young legs could carry him.

Ponniah was free! It was a long time before it was safe for him to return to his father's house. The whole village was related as only caste villages in India can be, family to family, and the hue and cry pursued him for many a day; but at last he got home again, and remained there till his people were ready to send him to school again.

While waiting, one day he heard an evangelist telling the story of Jesus Christ, the Lamb of God whose sacrifice taketh away the sins of the world. While Ponniah was not yet ready to leave home and wealth for that gospel, he believed the simple story, believed the severe yet joyful evangelist, and promised himself that some time he would turn to that "Way" and yield to that "Book." Sacrifice and persecution lay in that path.

Outside the village and a half mile away, upon a rising ground stood the village idol, a huge image of brick and mortar, covered with plaster and hideously fashioned and painted, some eighteen feet high, turning its great hollow eyesockets toward the village. On festal occasions the village clerk would place the big silver eyes, of which he was official custodian, within the hollow sockets, so their god might see and smile upon the village.

Ponniah and his friend Peria Swamy stood beside the idol and were speaking of the futility of idolatry. Ponniah said, "I don't believe in idols, and I do not fear them."

"Neither do I," said Peria Swamy.

"Watch me," said Ponniah, and he leaped lightly to the knees of the great idol, then climbed to its arm which was laid across the breast, then, standing upon the arm, he removed his sandal and slapped the big idol across the face with the most insulting object imaginable to Hindu thought, his leather shoe.

Now, Ponniah was not a Christian, he only hoped to become one some day, and yet he had thrown off the shackles of superstition so fully that he could renounce idolatry forever. Had he been a Christian, he would not have insulted the god his people worshiped. His action was seen and the village clerk determined to revenge the community insult and punish Ponniah. He sent for the inspector of police and informed him that Ponniah had stolen the big silver eyes of the idol.

In the house of the clerk the inspector questioned the clerk:

"You say that you saw him steal those eyes?" he asked.

"Yes, sir, I saw him steal them," he said.

"What were they like, Clerk?" asked the inspector.

"Sir, they were big silver balls, as big as your two fists," said the clerk.

"Papa," said his little son, who had come

"He removed his sandal and slapped the big idol across the face"

in unnoticed, "they aren't the balls you keep in that chest in the corner, are they?"

Then the big inspector looked in the chest, and there were the silver eyes, and Ponniah was proved innocent of the charge against him. He had again escaped danger.

But Ponniah was unpopular at home, and he slipped away to me and asked me to baptize him, as he wanted to be a Christian. I taught him to pray and in answer to his prayers he found peace and joy.

I asked the leaders of the church at Tuticorin if we should baptize him, and if they thought he would make a good Christian.

In the mat-walled church at Tuticorin he was baptized and stayed with me for a day or two while we were planning what he should do. The second night we lay asleep in my little room on the roof of a great grain warehouse, a little room I rented for one dollar and sixty-six cents a month, the only quarters I had for months at a time. I woke suddenly, for some one was fumbling at my feet.

"What do you want?" I asked.

"Where is that Pillay boy?" was the answer. I knew then that Ponniah's friends had come to take him away, for they were of high caste and felt his defection to Christianity most keenly.

"Get out of here," I shouted, and rose to pursue them. How they ran, and how I ran after them! But they made their escape, clattering down the three sets of stairs.

The next night, however, they found him while he was at supper, waited till he came out of the Hindu restaurant, then laid him forcibly inside an oxcart and tied him hand and foot. When they were not watching he slipped his hands from their bonds, untied his feet, and ran away in the darkness to me. Brother Rajappan and I placed him upon an early train to Madras, and he went away, assuring me with boyish confidence that he would study hard in the mission school there and thus become a great preacher.

So he stayed in Madras and studied as hard as he was able, grinding away at that beautiful but difficult Tamil poetry with its marvelous capacity of saying much in few words. There he learned the choice verse of Tiruvalluvar, who "was wont to hollow out a mustard seed and pour the Seven Seas inside it."

But his longing for home and mother overcame him. He had not yet found out that Christ is all in all. One evening, without my permission, he took the train southward and the next evening reached Tuticorin. Thence he traveled afoot to his village and his people. They welcomed him with open arms. He was glad to be at home again. His parents were the same dear parents he had left behind when he came to Christ. The evening passed, and Ponniah lay down to rest in the same cot he had used as a boy.

He woke suddenly, conscious that his mother was bending over him. "My son," she said, "we are so glad that you have come home. We have been disgraced by your falling into the evil way of the Christians, and now your father has brought the Brahman priest, the branding iron is red-hot, and we will brand your tongue to cleanse you from the pollution of baptism and of mingling with the accursed eaters of flesh and of kine. When thus you are clean once more, we shall take you back into caste, and you shall be our son again."

"But I cannot leave Jesus. He has saved

me." This was all he could say before his father's viselike grip was upon him and the hot branding-iron was before his eyes. He struggled, and they were frantic, but his youth conquered in the end, and when I saw him the following evening at my camp in a nearby village, he showed me his body clawed and bleeding as if some wild beast had met him. "The wounds," said he, "with which I was wounded in the house of my friends."

Then Ponniah went to a mission school in Tinnevelly, but one day the letters from home were too much for him, and one of them told him that his uncle was dying. Ponniah went home without my permission. He found the man lying upon a cot, and knelt beside him.

"Uncle," said he, "Jesus Christ has saved me from my sins, and I have peace with God. Do you believe he could save you too?"

"Of course, if he saved you. I never was as bad as you," was his uncle's answer.

"Uncle, may I pray for you?"

"Yes, if you want to, pray."

Then Ponniah prayed for his uncle, who had wronged him, had bound him, had beaten him, and would have prevented his education; and his prayer was like this: "O God, my uncle has worshiped idols all his life. He has bowed down to stocks and stones. Wilt thou not come into his heart and save him, for his heart has become like the stones he worshiped? O Jesus, come into his heart to-day."

While Ponniah prayed, Jesus was knocking at the stony portal of the old man's heart. It opened a little and the old man felt the warmth that had not been there for years, the warmth of love like the shining of the sun in springtime. It felt so good that he just threw the door wide open and Jesus came into his heart.

"O Ponniah, I've got it, I've got it," he shouted.

"What have you got, uncle?" asked Ponniah.

"I don't know what it is, Ponniah, but I think it's salvation," he said.

The death of the heathen is a most dismal affair. They crowd a great number of folks into the little room of the dying, and long before his spirit goes, the death wail is sounding through the whole village—that wail that chills the marrow of your bones, that tears your heart with its long-drawn agonies.

But Ponniah's uncle did not die that way.

He refused all mourners and Ponniah kept them away, and when he died, his spirit went with praise and joy unspeakable, went home to God. Ponniah came to tell me all about it. He said he had never heard of such a triumphant death, and read me a beautiful Tamil poem he had written describing it.

Ponniah came to me a month before I left for America, and gave me a deed for an acre and a half of land in his village. He has come into the possession of his own property at last, and with a smile he said, "I shall build a Methodist church building upon that land, and when you return to India, I want you to dedicate it."

Ponniah's last letter told of thirteen converts whom he had led into "the Way."

III

FOR THE BRITISH RAJ

THIRTEEN years ago, in a village of North India, I saw the two for the first time. I had jumped from the oxcart and with the *munshi* was walking toward the *mohulla* of the Christians. It was then that I saw the one, the elder. He stood at the entrance of the village street. Three silver medals hung from his quilted jacket. As I neared he stood sharply to attention, and threw up his hand in a military salute. Then I saw his face—a grizzled old veteran of the Indian army. You have seen the face of General Joffre? Darken it to a rich brown and dress it in an Indian turban, and you have my friend Thakur Das.

"Bandagi, Maharaj.[1] Welcome to our unworthy village. "*Hat!* Get back! Will you boys and girls trample the Maharaj

---

[1] Literally, "Great King."

that you crowd him so?"—and he descended on the naked children, unused to the sight of a fair-skinned *sahib* from afar.

I turned with a laugh. 'Twas then I saw the other. He was the leader of the array behind me, a boy of ten. He had been herding cows, and his long bamboo staff still lay on his shoulder. The cows were forgotten. He saw only me, and as I walked into the village I could have swung my hand behind my back and caught him by the arm.

"Maharaj will honor my house first. Run, Kanhai Singh, and bring some warm buffalo milk. Take this pice for sweetening in it."

The little cowherd came forward with hand outstretched for the money. His eyes were blazing with excitement and his bare limbs were quivering.

"I perceive you have seen the world somewhat, Thakur Das," and I studied the shining medals on his bosom. I had learned to recognize the ribboned clasps of many of the wars England has waged in the East. "I see the Punjab and Afghanistan. What is the other?"

"It is Burma, Huzúr," and the old man chuckled. The crowd had gathered. I had lighted a long-laid fuse. "You and I know the world, Maharaj. I have told these simpletons"—and he waved his hand indiscriminately over the heads of all—"I have been telling them the wonders and marvels of the world. But what can they understand? They are *ganwars*—they know nothing but mud-walls, grass-thatch, and cow dung. *We* have seen the world." He dominated the situation, and their submission was complete.

The buffalo milk in the polished brass *lota* was placed in my hands and the boy sat on his haunches at my feet, staring unashamed into my face. Thakur Das waited while I drank. I handed the *lota* to the boy. He bore it within and returned with a fan.

Thakur Das could restrain himself no longer. "You are here to confirm my words, your Presence. I have told these men of the world, of Calcutta and Bombay, of the great 'black water' and the ships. I have told them of Lord Roberts. He loved our regiment. I have seen him halt the sun in the heavens, when the Afghans were waiting for darkness to ambush us in the gorges. I have seen Lord Roberts hold up his hand like this, and call down thunder and lightning and rain till his enemies were paralyzed with fear, and he would capture them by thousands. Is it not so, Maharaj?"

I hesitated one small moment. "You have said it, Thakur Das," I answered.

" 'Tis so indeed. Ah, sir, the world is very large and wonderful. You and I have seen it."

He reached inside his quilted jacket and drew forth a little book, dirt-stained, thumb-marked, yet more precious than the gold of Ophir. A glance at it would show that it had been kept for years.

"Huzur, my certificates. Will you graciously read them and tell these what is written there."

I opened the book. Kanhai had stopped fanning. Faded pages and faded writing were pasted in an old copybook. They were certificates of good character, good service, and good will that Sipahi Thakur Das had managed to secure from officers of his regiment—the Sixteenth Rajputs. There was also his honorable discharge.

"But for my wound which took me to Peshawar, Lord Roberts would have given me one also," he added by way of apology as I closed the book.

It was his day of triumph long awaited. Why should I lessen the luster of it, or deprive this village Cæsar of his crown? The simple crowd came closer.

"Men of Tilaspur, I have read these certificates written by great officers of the British Raj—majors, captains, and lieutenants, men who know and understand the world. They portray my friend here, Thakur Das" (he was standing to attention as on a dress parade), "as a man highly respected by all who know him, a brave and loyal soldier of the great Queen-Empress. He has distinguished himself in every campaign and earned the gratitude of the Raj. In his retirement and old age he is worthy of your obedience, love, and reverence. And you, Kanhai Singh, be a blessing to your father in his last days."

As I spoke I saw another soldier, small but straight, standing to attention with a palm-leaf fan.

That night in the quiet mango grove where my tent was pitched I sat down to write. In the near distance the village had already sunk to rest. Suddenly upon the mango leaves beyond me appeared the shadows of three heads, followed by a quiet cough. I turned my head, feigning surprise:

"Well, Kanhai Singh, who are these you have brought with you?

"Maharaj, this is Daulat Ram, the son of the *lumbardar*. He is betrothed to my little sister, and is my brother. This is Baldeo, a *bhangi*, an outcaste and a Christian. My father does not know we play with him, but he can read, Maharaj, and he reads to us about the great world beyond out of his Second Reader. And so we let him play with us, sometimes, when the *dal* field yonder is the world and we go to see its sights. He must stay far behind when we attack the Afghans, lest perchance he should be wounded, and we should have to bring him in." A shiver ran through his frame.

"You are cold, Kanhai, and the evening is warm—"

"No, your Presence, I was thinking of the beating our fathers would give us if we carried Baldeo in. Yonder, Sahib"—he was gathering confidence with every moment and unburdening his little heart—"yonder on that mound near that old well Lord Roberts sits and watches us attack. O Sahib, just three days ago Lord Roberts with his own hand pinned a medal on me here," and he touched his breast.

I laughed. "How could he do that, Kanhai, when you wear no shirt or coat?"

My laugh hurt him and he wilted like a sensitive plant.

"I do see it now, Kanhai. You must have been a very brave soldier and done a marvelous deed to have earned such honor."

"Yes, Sahib, I killed three thousand Afghans in one hour, and Lord Roberts said 'twas well done. He had been watching me, you see, Sahib, watching all the time. Maharaj," and the boy sat down at my feet, innocence and boldness combined. "Will you take me with you into the great world?" His eyes, his whole face, pleaded with his words.

"No, Kanhai, you are but a boy now. You must grow tall and strong. You must tend your father too, you know."

"Yes, Sahib," and he lowered his voice, "but my heart here tells me the Afghans will be all gone before I grow big, Lord Roberts may be dead, and where then shall my medals come from?"

"There will be plenty of Afghans left, my boy, and plenty of medals too. But they are given only to the truthful and obedient. Now you may go, all three of you."

He half rose, but bent again, and touched my shoe with his brown forehead:

"Maharaj, may I speak? May I utter one request." His black eyes were pouring forth the intensities within; from their craters the deep fires below leaped out.

"What is it, Kanhai? I will do anything that is good for you, my son."

"A certificate," he whispered.

"Of course," I answered, and I wrote: "This is to certify that Kanhai Singh, son of Thakur Das, is a brave lad, honest and obedient. He will some day, I doubt not, be a great and good man."

He held out his hand for the folded paper, and could not keep back the laughter. He held the priceless document close against his heart, and bowed to the earth once more.

"Where will you keep it, Kanhai?" I dared not risk another jest about that little brown body.

"In the inner band of my green cap that I wear when I go to the fairs. No one will know that I keep it there, Maharaj."

He was gone and I turned again to my letter: "Even these little villages of India are touched by the movements of the world. There is no sight more interesting than to watch the first ripples of our world-civilization striking these quiet shores."

All this was thirteen years ago. Lying undisturbed it had grown dusty in the pigeon-holes of memory. It would be lying so yet but for an accident.

I had missed my train at a wayside station. In my impatience I paced the graveled platform. A train from the south came slowly in and halted. Suddenly I was aroused with curiosity.

"Babu, what train is this, all third-class carriages, and guarded with soldiers?"

"Sir, it is a train of wounded returning to their homes," answered the station master.

The doors opened and eleven men were lifted out by gentle hands and deposited on the station platform. Some were lying on light stretchers, others were sitting up, one or two could even stand.

In far-off India the wreckage of the storm in Flanders! It seemed unreal, untrue. No quarrel of theirs, but theirs the sightless eyes, the amputated limbs, the torn features, the shattered frames. These were the hopelessly mangled—the ashes of the furnace.

They laid the last one taken out near my feet. It was not till the train pulled out that I heard him speaking to another:

"The long journey is all but over. Home,

Shankar, home! Bear up, brother! What honor they will give us in our villages! And when our medals come—ah then—"

I looked at the man who had spoken; the voice sounded strangely familiar. The man was sitting on his stretcher, sergeant's stripes on his left sleeve. I could not see the face under the large khaki turban. He was speaking again as I stepped around to a place more advantageous:

"Eh, Dilawar Singh, why such moaning? Think you that you are the only man wounded that you act the woman? Shankar here is torn far worse than you. He lies quiet when he is not laughing."

I was standing now behind Dilawar Singh. The sergeant raised his eyes to me. A moment of perplexity—then the flash of mutual recognition. I saw my village lad of years gone by.

"O Sahib, my Sahib," he cried in joy. "Do I see you once more in a dream, as I have seen you so often, or is it yourself indeed?"

I rushed to him and kneeling took his hand:

"Kanhai Singh, my son, you are wounded. Tell me how badly."

"It is nothing, Sahib, nothing. Just enough to keep me from my regiment and from France." There was the same intensity in his look, and the same expression of high resolve. My cowherd had but become a man.

"He is wounded worse than any of us," spoke the soldier lying next him.

"It is untrue, Sahib. I can sit up, you see. Shankar here will never sit again."

"Tell me how it happened, Kanhai Singh"—but the attendants had now arrived and were lifting his stretcher.

"If you will come with me a little way in the *baili,* Sahib, I will tell you all. But that is asking much."

"Not too much," I answered, and followed him to the waiting oxcart that was to take him to his village. "I will go with you to your home. Is your father yet alive?"

"Still living, Sahib, but very old. When he heard that war had broken out and that my regiment was going he was bent on reenlisting. That could not be of course, but he came to see me off, and blessed me as a soldier of the Raj."

On that journey I heard the story in all its details from the lips of the wounded man:

"We began intrenching under fire, Sahib. The men were unused to it. They were like little children when the monsoon breaks and the thunder-claps are near. So many fell. I kept thinking of my father and Lord Roberts. So I kept our company to its task. For that they gave me this" —and he pointed to his sergeant's stripes. Then followed many a story of camp and trench. He drew near to the end:

"One day at Shahvanshi [Givenchy], Sahib—I cannot get those French names well—I received this wound. 'Tis well it is no worse. We were crowded in our trenches to repel an attack. How little we suspected they were mined. Suddenly the Germans exploded them. I can remember the noise. I tried to rise, to hold our line, but it grew so dark I could not see. Some one fell upon me. The rest I have forgotten."

Down went the sun, a ball of fire. It would soon be dark. For a long time now we had been silent, each thinking his own thoughts, each dreading what lay ahead. Finally he broke the silence:

"Yonder behind those *babool* trees lies our little village. From France to Tilaspur—'tis a long and painful journey, Sahib."

"Yes, see the boys of your village. You will know them. Even so you met me years ago."

"Kanhai Singh has come back! Kanhai Singh has come back! And an English Sahib is with him."

Back to the village the cry was carried by a score of boyish voices. The sound swept through the village. They ran together from all its *mohullas*. The men and women returning from the fields hastened their steps, wondering what the shouting was about. Perhaps some highway robbers had been caught. Perhaps some quarrel had occurred and bamboo *lathis* were raining down on naked heads. Children in troops formed the advance guard, rushing out. Behind them hurried the men, bewildered and questioning. The women ran as fast as the jewelry on their ankles and the babies on their hips would allow, peeping all the while from close-drawn *chadars*. The crowd surrounded us. Kanhai Singh greeted them cheerily.

Down the road came Thakur Das, an old man now. He had stopped to pin on his medals. Perplexity was written on his face.

Again the military salute and the word of welcome. Then the eager searching of the father's eye:

"Leap down, Kanhai Singh! How is it you sit up there when the Maharaj is down and on his feet? Have you forgotten your manners, boy?"

"Let him rest. Your son is wounded, Thakur Das. Order a *khatiya* and take him down tenderly."

The father's eyes narrowed as he renewed the search. His son looked sound enough sitting covered by the *razai*.

"Where did the ball take you, my son? All soldiers are wounded at some time. I too bear my scars."

"Your son is wounded, Thakur Das"

The *khatiya* had come, and we lifted him gently from the oxcart. The movement undid the *razai,* and for one moment uncovered the limbs. The father's quick eye caught their message.

"*Hae! Hae!*" he screamed, and threw his arm before his eyes, as if the sight had blinded him. "He will never walk again. Hae! Hae! Both gone! Both gone! My son! My only son!

The wailing was caught up by the gathered crowd and the little village gave itself unrestrainedly to sorrow. Kanhai Singh and I alone were quiet. I turned to Thakur Das:

"Thakur Das, you are a soldier and a veteran, as well as a father. You can be steady under fire, and you can be steady under affliction. You are a hero and have been honored—your son is a hero too, and must be honored in a way more fitting. What welcome is this to give him who has given his strength in the service of the Raj?"

The father quieted his sobs, but still looked the picture of unutterable woe.

"Father" (the voice was very steady),

"I bring to you the personal greetings and salaams of Lord Roberts. I saw him with these eyes of mine and heard his voice. He inspected our regiment five weeks before I was wounded, and asked if the sons of any of his veterans were in the ranks. I stepped forward. He came and spoke to me, and bade me carry to you his greetings. I have done so."

Thakur Das had heard with head bowed low. He raised himself to his full height.

"Son, you have paid lightly for this honor. Let me hear no sigh of regret pass your lips. The village shall know of it."

Then turning to the crowd he shouted, his voice stern, but trembling with emotion: "Silence! Bid this foolish wailing cease! Is this our answer to Lord Roberts' greeting?"

As they bore him to his wife and to his mother, I overheard their conversation:

"Kanhai, you and I now understand how all things are. We know the world."

"We have seen the world, my father."

IV

THE TIGER AND THE LAMB

ONE afternoon I was sitting in the home of Sister Martha in the little Indian village of Keela Karanthai. The reason we called her Martha was that whenever the pastor came to that village she was always so busy getting dinner for the pastor that she could not get out to the morning service, and so when I baptized her "Martha" the whole congregation smiled. We have to change their names in many cases because the old names are associated with odious aspects of heathenism.

In one corner of the little house the cattle were tied, munching away at their stalks of millet fodder, Sister Martha was cooking in another corner, and a number of the members of the congregation were seated around me on the floor, listening to my stories about Christ and about America, until I got tired of talking and excused myself on the ground that I had to write some letters. So I took out my fountain pen and began to write.

They watched in silence for some time, and then one nudged another and said in a whisper, "Appa, where does he get that ink?"

The other answered: "That isn't ink. That is a pencil."

But the first insisted, "It is ink; I can see it glisten."

Then the first said: "Haven't you any manners? Don't bother the missionary. He wants to write. Let him alone."

And I thought, "If they have too much politeness to ask me where I get the ink from a fountain pen, I will just let them be polite," and went on writing.

Very soon I found that they were far more polite than I, for I heard them saying, "That man is going to the city and will return again soon," and I butted right into their conversation and asked, "What man?"

In response they covered their mouths with their hands, and one answered, "Sh! —you must not speak his name!"

"But," said I, "how can I speak his name if you do not tell me his name?"

Seeing my lack of manners, they took me by the hand and led me clear outside of the village. Nobody tells secrets inside of an Indian village, for the houses are jammed so close together that what you say in this house can be heard in the third house away, so they always take people outside the village to talk secrets.

When we got some distance away from town, under a spreading banyan tree, they looked around for possible eavesdroppers, and seeing none, Channiah said in a whisper, "Iya, his name is Pakkia Nathan!"

"Well," said I, "that is very interesting."

"Yes," he answered, "he is a very dangerous man."

Another added, "Iya, he has ten sons bigger than himself, and he is a tremendous big fellow with a chest as big as a barrel and great big fists."

From consequent remarks I gathered that they were approximately the size of hams.

"Sir," said another, "they are the terror

of the whole community and many villages near here. We never even mention their names, for we fear they will burn our houses down as they have burned many houses down before this. They have committed all manner of crimes, and these eleven are just the nucleus of the gang of scoundrels that terrorize the country."

Now, the more they told me about Pakkia Nathan, the more certain I felt that I did not wish to have anything to do with him or any member of his family. I regarded them as undesirable acquaintances for any Methodist minister, even though only a missionary.

The next morning I was leaving the village, and although I had spoken late the night before, nearly the whole congregation came along to say good-by. There is an etiquette which prevails in South India, and in following it, I generally allow them all to come several blocks distance outside the village, and then, turning around and bowing very low, say, "Salaam." The whole congregation says, "Salaam," and remains standing there. The missionary walks a few paces away and again turns toward the waiting people and says, "Salaam," and the congregation again says, "Salaam," and after repeating this ceremony five or six times, it is quite fitting for the missionary to enter his oxcart and drive away.

Brother Cook, of our South India Conference, says that the Indian oxcart greatly resembles the American "Ford." The minor differences, he says, are entirely lost in the striking similarities. The oxcart has only two cylinders, but you seize both these cylinders by the tail, and crank the tails. By continual cranking you can secure a speed of three miles an hour, but that is the speed limit. When you cease cranking, they drop back to two miles, which is very slow for an American.

I was just about to enter this machine and speed away at three miles an hour when I saw around the end of the cart a very hearty-looking man approaching, and I knew at once that it was Pakkia Nathan, and I did not want to see him or speak with him at all. Just at that moment, however, it seemed to me that the Lord said very clearly, "Tell

Pakkia Nathan that unless he repents of his sins he will be lost forever."

My knees began to knock together and my heart thumped in a most disagreeable manner. The congregation had disappeared from behind me, but I learned long ago not to fear any man so much as God, and I walked up to Pakkia Nathan and said to him, "Pakkia Nathan, if all that I hear about you is true, and you do not repent of your many great crimes, God will send you to hell."

Natives of India have very clear notions about hell. You need not prove its existence by philosophy or theology, for they believe in a hell as thoroughly as any that Dante ever imagined and depicted; and I looked Pakkia Nathan over as I spoke, noted his fine figure, his splendid bearing, his muscles chiseled like those of a Hercules, though he was not nearly so large as I had expected; and I longed for his conversion and salvation. I said, "I don't want you to be lost, Pakkia Nathan, and I am going to pray for you. Come along with me while I pray for you."

Then I seated myself in the oxcart and he held the side of it and leaned over while I prayed: "O God, this man has committed every crime that the world knows anything about, and his hands are stained with his iniquities, and his heart is black with his sins. Hear my prayer, for Jesus' sake, and touch his wicked heart, and wash him in the blood of the Lamb."

Now, while I was talking with God about him, I almost forgot how near he was to me, and when I looked up, was startled to see him gazing intently into my eyes.

"Go away," he said, "and come back again."

And I went. I did not want to argue with Pakkia Nathan.

It was two weeks or more before I got back to Keela Karanthai, and as I drew near the village, I saw Pakkia Nathan coming out to meet me. Though he was large and muscular, he had the litheness and grace that you see in the tiger, a magnificent combination of power and ease of motion, and I got out of my oxcart to meet him. He was running till he halted before me.

"Sir, I have been thinking of what you said," he cried.

I thought, "Surely I am in for trouble now."

"And I have decided," he continued, "to become a Christian."

If some old tiger had walked out of the jungle and said, "I have decided to become an ox. Kindly put a yoke on my neck and hitch me up to a plow," I should have been no more surprised.

"Pakkia Nathan, do you mean it?"

"Yes," he answered. "I have been talking with the native pastor in the village, and I have given my heart to Christ, and he has forgiven me my sins."

And what he said was true. God had forgiven him his sins and cleansed him from them, and given him the gift of the Spirit. We took him into the church, and he is the leader of our Board of Stewards in that village to this day.

A few weeks later, on the day I received him into the church, he asked me to wait a few minutes and brought his ten sons whom he placed before me.

"What do they want?" I asked, for those big black fellows looked very much like a thunder cloud.

"They all wish to be Christians too," said he. We took them all in, and the family of Pakkia Nathan, with his wife and his sons and their wives, and their children, came to over forty, and became a very important addition to the church in that village.

A few weeks later I came to the village and spent the Sabbath there. After preaching in the morning I wished to go to a nearby village, Vembur, and preach there in the afternoon, and suggested to Pakkia Nathan that I wished him to come along too. He said he would be glad to come, if I would only wait a little while, and I consented.

Back he came with his ten big sons, and I asked him, "What do they want now?"

"Sir," he said with a smile, "they want to go along and preach too."

As we drew near Vembur the people of the village saw us coming and knew us from afar. How often we suffer by keeping bad company! They knew Pakkia Nathan and all his gang, or thought they did, and when we got into Vembur there was no one to preach to. They had all gone into their houses and locked the doors, and even the windows were barred. There was not one movable object on the street, except an ox-cart and the oxen were not hitched to that or it also would have been taken away.

When I saw the emptiness, I said, "Pakkia Nathan, you have scared them all away. You will have to get them back. Sing for them, Pakkia Nathan."

Now you can have no conception of the way he sang unless you can conceive of a great pipe organ singing words instead of the bare notes. Out of his deep chest, with a mighty voice, he sang one of our simple Christian lyrics set to a tune that all South India knows:

> "Praise Jesus, O my soul!
> The spotless Son of God!
> Who came from heaven and earth
> To save us from our sins!
> Praise Jesus, only
> Jesus, O my soul!"

He had hardly finished the first stanza when the windows were unbarred and folks

"Pakkia Nathan, you have scared them all away"

were looking out, and before he had ceased singing, the doors were opened wide and the crooked narrow streets were jammed full of people. As I looked over the crowd I said, "Pakkia Nathan, get up on the wagon, and preach to them," and he did.

"O you people," he said in a musical voice that was almost singing, "you were afraid of me. You were afraid of my big sons. You needn't be afraid of us any more. We will not harm you any more. We will try to do good now instead of evil, for God has taken away the fierce tiger-hearts and given us all the hearts of little lambs. We will try to make up for our wickedness of the past, for Jesus has saved us."

He and his sons earn their living now by honest toil, and are greatly respected, and whenever I want to start a revival among people of his caste in some new heathen village, I get him to take one of his sons and go there for a few days. The revival always starts when he tells how his tiger-heart was changed.

V

A MISSION SCHOOL ROMANCE

THE young Wellesley graduate had been in India just three years, and found herself now in charge of the American Mission High School at Walayatpur. She was seated in the veranda of the bungalow after her early morning *chhoti haziri* of tea and toast. School had just closed for the *truly* hot weather (170° in the sun). It was the first of May, and the young lady from Wellesley found her thoughts about evenly divided between the May Days of old, when she had been "queen," and the girls of her graduating class whose "futures" now presented a present problem.

A slight shuffling of feet—repeated to attract attention—brought her out of her thoughts. She turned her head and saw Shanti Masih, one of her "fair girl graduates." The girl was the brightest and most attractive in her class—one of the finest the school had ever known.

"Well, Shanti, I am still rejoicing in your great success in the government examination. *First* in the provinces out of seventeen hundred candidates—and ahead of all the boys! It's just lovely! You ought to be in Wellesley."

"Miss Sahiba, that is in line with what I have come to talk over with you. I want to go on, and be somebody—*do* something. We Indian women *can,* and I'm so glad that our day is at last dawning."

"So you don't wish to get married, like Piyari, and Nirmalini, and others of your class?"

"No, Miss Sahiba, *I* want to study some more."

And so they talked, and it was settled that Shanti should take her college course at the Isabella Thoburn College at Lucknow, and then perhaps go to America for a Ph.D.

"What a pity," thought the young missionary from the West, "that Shanti has neither father nor mother to share in our rejoicing over her success! But, then, she's a Christian, and they were Hindus. They must have perished in the great famine."

Just then a man was seen entering the mission compound. As he came closer the missionary noted that he was a hunchback. He made straight for the veranda, and when he stopped at the foot of the steps, the missionary saw that his face was scarred by deep marks of smallpox, and that he was very dirty, though apparently not of the lowest caste of Hindus. He appeared to be about fifty years old. Looking at the missionary, he said:

"I have come for my wife."

"For your wife!" exclaimed the missionary. "We do not keep people's wives around here—this is a girls' school."

"I know that," said he. "I was told by the lawyer that she was in this school. He said you would have to give her to me."

"We give you a wife? Never!"

"If not," said the man, strangely confident, "then I'll *take* her!"

He seated himself, unbidden, on the top step of the veranda, and took out from the inner folds of his clothes several papers wrapped in a greasy, smoky, fly-specked piece of oilcloth. With these before him, he said:

"I have here the legal papers, signed and properly attested, showing that I was betrothed according to our Hindu rites to Mohini Sarkar twelve years ago. The famine several years ago separated me from the girl's family, but almost as by chance I got trace of an uncle of the girl and have finally learned that the girl was left here by her parents during the famine and is now known as Shanti Masih."

The hunchback looked at the missionary to note the effect of his words. The lady sat and stared, as if she had lost the power of speech. It was her own dear Shanti that this unsightly creature was demanding! Married twelve years ago, when she was only six!

Finally she summoned the *mali* (gardener), who was leading the oxen to the well to draw water, and told him to go and call the Christian *munshi* who gave her her daily lesson in the vernacular.

When the *munshi* appeared, the missionary asked him to read aloud the documents, and as he did so her heart sank. There seemed to be no question as to the purport of the papers.

"Are those papers genuine, Munshiji?" asked the missionary.

"There is no doubt about it," he replied in English. "They bear the proper seals and stamps."

"Thank you," she said. "I don't need to trouble you further."

When the *munshi* was gone, the missionary said to the beggar: "I must talk with our missionaries about this. You may call again at three o'clock this afternoon."

"May I not see the girl now?" he asked.

"No," came the firm reply, as the door closed and he was left on the veranda.

The missionary did some rapid thinking; then she wrote and sent a note to the principal of the high school for young men, asking him to come over and take tiffin at two o'clock instead of dinner at seven-thirty, as there was a question of great importance to discuss.

Then she tried to read, but could not keep

her mind on the subject. At the top of each page was the sweet face of Shanti, and at the bottom, always, the unsightly figure of the hunchback. Under the spur of her emotion she was able to dash off some appealing letters to her patrons.

One thing she did *not* do—and that was to call in Shanti to talk it over. How could she *ever* do that!

Just at ten o'clock, as breakfast had been announced, a rumble of wheels was followed by a call—"Any Americans around here?"

The missionary stepped out on to the front veranda to find a middle-aged man, with a smiling face, looking out at the door of the *theka gari* (hackney carriage). She invited him in, introducing him to her three assistant teachers who had already answered the call to breakfast.

The curry and rice was made to cover five plates instead of four, some more tamarind juice was added to the large water jug, and the *mali* was told to bring in another papaya from the tree near the well. The breakfast was a success.

The American visitor—a Christian business man out to appraise the value of missionary work, proved to be excellent company. He liked the Indian teachers, and did not find them as shy as he had anticipated! One thing he took care to do—to announce that he had come to see things, but *not to give money!*

The school was inspected, and then he drove on to see the great Hindu temple and the unusually fine bazaar. He was asked to return at two o'clock and take tiffin, when the other missionary would be present.

The tiffin table was surrounded at two-thirty, and the hostess then introduced the subject of the hunchback. The globe-trotter was intensely interested. The missionary principal of the boys' school looked worried. The Indian teachers showed the deepest pain and concern on their faces. All agreed that if the papers were genuine, there seemed little hope for poor Shanti. It was explained to the gentleman from America that the marriage laws of both Hindus and Mohammedans were absolutely valid in British courts of justice.

Three o'clock had struck when the *khid-*

matgar (table servant) announced that a cripple beggar was demanding to see the Miss Sahiba. The poor missionary looked white and scared, and very tired.

The principal of the boys' school left the room, saying he would have a talk with the hunchback.

The man from America asked to see Shanti, his curiosity and sympathy having been aroused by all he had heard.

In a short time the principal returned, saying that it was a hopeless case—the hunchback was determined to follow up his legal rights.

It was then that the stranger from America proposed that they all go out on to the veranda and see the hunchback. For himself, he wished to say something to the beggar, and he would like Shanti to be his interpreter.

The missionary stepped swiftly to his side, and whispered,

"Don't tell her!"

On the veranda the American visitor, through Shanti's able interpretation, got out of the hunchback many details of his past life, even getting him to disclose his sordid plans for the woman who might become his wife. It was a shocking revelation, to all except Shanti herself, as to what awaited the fairest product of the mission school.

Then the hunchback cut things short by producing the papers, saying: "I demand my rights! Where is the girl?"

It was a tense moment. Every countenance was worth studying. The missionary's face was pale with dread, and her eyes were fixed on Shanti. The principal's eyes blazed, and as he looked at the hunchback there took shape a grim determination to fight this thing to the finish. One assistant teacher sank into a chair, her face buried in her hands, while the two others drew close to Shanti, as if to protect her. Shanti herself could not understand what was happening, and looked in perplexity from one to another. The hunchback's look was bold, and with each added second of silence he was gaining confidence, yet there lurked in his eyes a fear lest by some trick he should yet lose his rights. The visitor's face was calm and confident.

It was the stranger from America who broke the silence, saying, "Now, ladies and gentlemen, watch a real American 'disappearing trick,' whereby the hunchback is made to vanish into thin air."

His levity was not appreciated.

"Ask this miserable creature, Miss Shanti," continued he, "how much money a wife would be worth to him."

The hunchback looked perplexed, as Shanti interpreted. "Ask him how many rupees he would be willing to take *instead* of a wife."

Light began to dawn on the entire group, including the hunchback. He had heard a good deal of America, that land of wealth, where *lakhpatis* (millionaires) lived in every town, and he began to do some figuring.

"Five rupees a month," he said to himself—"that would make sixty rupees a year, a comfortable income; and for ten years—that's six hundred rupees." He had made a great flight of imagination and risen to a dizzy height of mathematics! He announced: "She is worth six hundred rupees to me. I ask six hundred."

The visitor pulled out his American pocketbook.

"Put down," said he through his young interpreter, "your legal papers."

The hunchback put them on the veranda, within easy reach of himself.

"Now," said the visitor, "I put down six hundred rupees beside them," and he put down six crisp Government of India notes, each for one hundred rupees. Then he went on, looking fixedly at the hunchback, as the surprised Shanti translated his words:

"You take this six hundred rupees, leave your marriage papers on the veranda, and go out at that gate—never to show your face here again!"

The hunchback did not budge, but covered his papers with his hand.

"I demand *money,*" he said.

"What!" exclaimed the visitor, "is he not satisfied with the bargain?"

The group on the veranda smiled, while the principal said, "Yours is paper money; he asks for silver."

The missionary, her face flushed with gratitude as she looked at her American

"Ask this miserable creature how much money a wife would be worth to him"

visitor, started for the door, saying: "I can manage it. The salary for the school staff has just come to-day from the bank. It is in silver."

She ran to the safe, and a moment later came out with a crocheted bag made of strong white cotton cord. From it were taken six hundred silver rupees, and counted out on the veranda.

The hunchback's eyes glistened. The visitor shoved the six piles over toward him.

"Now you take it—and get!" he exclaimed.

"Get what?" inquired Shanti, puzzled, just how to translate the expression.

"Get out!" said he with real emphasis.

The hunchback gathered up the coins. He rolled them in a long wad, and, with the extra folds of his *dhoti* (long loin cloth), bound them around his waist. Then he made a salaam that took in the entire group on the veranda, and was gone.

As he disappeared through the gateway the American visitor thanked Miss Shanti for her excellent service as interpreter, who laughingly replied—

"The hunchback really disappeared!"

When the American globe-trotter left that night after a genuine Indian *pilau* dinner, he said to the missionary: "Don't tell Shanti! That pleasure I reserve for myself. I'll tell her—in America, when she comes to get her Ph.D."

As he settled himself in the carriage, he said aloud to himself, "Never spent two hundred dollars to better advantage in my life!"

VI

WHEN THE GODS ARE DYING

I. The Village

"THE company is starting already and the leading oxcarts are moving out of the village. Why dost thou tarry, Chajju, my son? The holy Mother Ganga[1] is far from here; wouldst thou take the long journey alone? I fear for the many *dakus*[2] along the way, who handle the lonely pilgrim as the hawk handles the chick. Go with thy fellow villagers and give thy mother's heart sweet peace."

Chajju bent his head and looked long at the ground before he made reply: "I am not worthy, my mother, to look with these sinful eyes of mine upon holy Ganga, nor to bathe in her sacred waters. Did not our neighbor, Mangal Sain, contract the leprosy by angering the fair goddess? Did not the sore eyes of Jitu develop into blindness, all

[1] The River Ganges. [2] Robbers.

because he would have them healed in Ganga water, knowing not how great the sin that sat upon him? Ganga smote him for his boldness. No, mother, ask me not to go this

year on pilgrimage to the bathing *teohar*.[1] For many months I have sinned exceedingly and my burden of guilt presses me down. It presses me down, mother, till my heart

[1] Festival.

is bent with the load, and I stagger along. I would atone by offerings at our village temple. Let Mahadev[1] forgive me, ere, as a pilgrim at the river, I pray the prayers of the pious and pour out holy libations, praising the name of Ganga."

"My son, thy words are not the words of comfort. How can I wait another year. Ere Mahadev forgive thy sin, thy mother may be far hence. I follow thy father on the long pilgrimage of Awagawan.[2] My heart too is heavy, knowing not what lies ahead. Speak not to me of the weight of guilt. Guilt is but clay to carry where dread is stone. Go name my name to Mother Ganga, and bid her be gracious to me on my long journey. Bring me the sacred water that I may offer it to Mahadev, and have strong protection from the *dakus* that infest the roads of eternity. O son, ere thou bear my ashes to the sacred river, bear my heart thither. Go and Ganga will not smite thee, for thy mother's sake! Ganga is woman, and Ganga understands."

Chajju walked toward the entrance of

[1] The Great God (Siva). [2] Transmigration.

the courtyard, then turned and came back. "Mother, I am still unpersuaded. Thou shalt have Ganga water. Our fellow villagers who go shall bring it to thee. My cousin, thy nephew, shall speak of thee to the goddess. Thy soul shall be at peace when it goes hence. . . . Why wouldst thou slay thy son, and drive him forth ahead of thee upon the lonely ways of death? The gods, O mother, are quick to destroy the unholy. The gods fill heaven and earth; the gods create terror in man's heart. I know I shall be slain for my presumption, or have some dreadful issue of my journey. Let my soul first be at peace; only thus can peace come to thee from me."

His mother sank to his feet, and covered her face with her hands. "Chajju, I see nothing but darkness before me. I had hoped to have light ahead. As on the sacred waters the lamps go drifting to the sea, so I had hoped to float down the river of time with light burning in my heart. But thou hast blown it out. O son, I sit in darkness. Who is my nephew when thou art my son? Who will bring comfort when thou hast brought sorrow?" She looked up into his face. "When I dandled thee a babe in my arms and nursed thee at this breast, then I said, 'This is my Saviour. Through this man-child the woman in me will be redeemed. My *karma*[1] is good. The road of motherhood is rough and painful, yet if it be the motherhood of men, it brings one to fair cities. I shall be blessed in him.' And so I sang thee happy songs and my heart overflowed with laughter. And so I praised the gods and taught thy baby lips to praise them too. 'Great is Mahadev! Great is Hanuman! Great is Ganesh!' I can hear thee yet speak thus in thy baby prattle." She leaped to her feet and continued: "Am I undone by this very praise I taught thee? Have I so filled thy heart with fear that thou fearest to redeem thy mother? ***Hae! Hae!*** the lot of woman is hard, so dependent on man is she! When man fails her, then is she ruined. This was my hour of hope, Chajju, but thou hast dashed it to the ground. Dying in my despair I shall be born woman again, ever woman to the end

[1] Lot.

of Awagawan.[1] Never, never shall I find release—"

She broke out in bitter weeping. Chajju laid his hand tenderly upon her shoulder: "My heart is crushed by thy sobs, my mother. Great are the gods, but great is a man's love for his mother. I obey thy word. For thee I risk the anger of holy Ganga. I go, mother. I shall confess at every shrine along the way, and give alms to every holy man I meet. Perchance at the end of the journey I shall have rid me of my load." He stood a moment looking off in deep thought, then his whole face lit up with his emotion: "And what if at the journey's end Mother Ganga should be pleased with *me,* and give me peace as well? O mother, with what adoration of her name I shall step into the sacred stream! With what praise I shall lift the water in my opened palms and pour it forth an offering! With what prayer I shall dip beneath the wave till I am covered by her presence and altogether in her power! Then shall I name thy name to her, and bring thee of her presence in this jar. . . .

[1] Transmigration.

Look: the oxcarts are not yet beyond the dal fields. I shall overtake them ere they reach the mango grove."

II. The City

In the street of an Indian city many were coming and going. Cheerful greetings of "*Rám! Rám!*" passed from lip to lip. The spirit of the *teohar*[1] was abroad. Two young men easily recognized as students of the Government College met, seemingly by appointment, at the crossing near the *banya's* shop, and joined the stream of carts and people flowing toward the river.

"A holiday, Hari Singh! Praise to the good God that made men Hindus, Mohammedans, and Christians, that we who study in the schools might have Hindu holidays and Mohammedan holidays and Christian holidays. If all were Hindus, then should we have to study so much the harder. Let us pray the gods to preserve all unbelievers."

"Did I hear you speak of the gods, Basant Ram? Since when have you become so in-

[1] Festival.

terested in them? We are Aryas,[1] you know—"

"Not the gods, Hari Singh, but holidays, that is where my interest lies to-day. But as for the gods, they are but names for the One, the All-Supreme. I am Hindu and I am Arya. I have been to worship this morning, which you have not; so am I better Hindu than you. I shall be a holy one long before you are."

Hari Singh laughed heartily and with folded hands bowed in mock adoration. "Holy indeed! I worship the feet of this Holy One! Worship in the morning and villainy all day. Such is your program. And now you go forth to enjoy the bathing festival, because there is pleasure in it, and yet in your heart there is despising of this superstitious folly. So does the Holy One offer the purchase money to Folly that he may wed his daughter Sport."

"Why, what a muddy philosopher you are, Hari Singh! If you had been to worship this morning your brain would be more settled. You talk as if you were not headed

[1] A Reform Sect in Hinduism, very strong in North India.

for the river. Your brain seems traveling backward to the city to sit in pious meditation throughout this holiday, while your feet keep ever stepping forward with the crowds. Did we create this bathing festival? No.

It has been given us and a holiday along with it. Let us enjoy life's gifts. Which is the wiser, Hari Singh—to despise a thing and yet enjoy it, or to despise a thing and lose some pleasure?"

Hari Singh, still dissimulating humility, answered, softly: "I am no philosopher, Basant Ram, yet I take it, Holy One, that you would have me this day enjoy that which I despise. Doing this, shall I attain to wisdom?"

Basant Ram laughed. "Hari Singh, sometimes I have great hopes for you. You are not so stupid as you seem. This must be a day of learning—call it not a holiday" —he heaved a sigh—"I must give my precious time to teaching you a lesson. You must know that there are many things that may be despised and yet enjoyed."

"And what are they, O Philosopher?"

"The women at the river bank, the precincts of the temple, the dice, and"—he looked around him as he spoke—"and these simpletons of the villages who throng the roads."

A look of disgust came over the face of his companion.

"And how will you enjoy these simpletons who do nothing but kick up the dust as they move along and choke themselves and us with it? There is no enjoyment from such as these. They are choked with their own ignorance and superstition. I despise them."

"Blind as ever, Hari Singh, you have yourself answered your own question. You will never pass the government examinations in spite of your long hours of study. One lobe of your brain is filled with deep knowledge of the sciences and the English classics, but the other, I weep to say it, is black with ignorance. One half of your mentality is kept in *pardah*[1] and never sees the world. The scales of your mind are uneven, Hari Singh, they do not weigh truth with any accuracy."

"Basant Ram, your words are covered with the dust of these countless feet. Would that Mother Ganga would wash you too, though you believe not in her reputed efficacy."

Basant Ram smiled again. "That is the point, Hari Singh. Let us enjoy the dust. '*Quod erat demonstrandum,*' as we say in mathematics. Let us enjoy their ignorance and their crude faith in Ganga and the gods. Let us have sport with that which we despise. So may we be good Arya missionaries, teaching the truth, and at the same

[1] The veil, the seclusion of Indian women.

time suck some sweetness out of the holiday. See here is a village company coming down the dirt road from the East. Look, Hari Singh, at the man who walks in front; some Buddhu or Chajju of a distant village. See how set his face, how rapt his look. He walks as in a dream. The vision of Mother Ganga is upon him. Poor fool! He is our man. Let us tell him what Hindus of to-day should believe. Hari Singh, share your new learning with this village enthusiast and see the look on his face change. Lift him and dip him in the waters of knowledge and pour out libations to truth on his behalf. It will be good for him, for knowledge is cleansing, and it will furnish us entertainment till we reach the crowded river bank and find sport more exciting."

Hari Singh caught his companion by the arm and shook him playfully as he replied: "Basant Ram, it would be well for these pilgrims that you get not too close to the water to-day, for at sight of you Ganga would flow backward to the mountains whence she came."

WHEN THE GODS ARE DYING

III. The Village Again

Large is the debt of gratitude that India owes to November. May and June torment her with hot winds and scorching sunlight; July, August, and September drench her with rain; October shakes her with ague and fever; but November lifts her up, puts strength into her limbs, adorns her with rich garments, paints her dark eyelids, and sets her forth the fairest daughter of the East, ravishing man's eye with her beauty and compelling his heart to love.

It was a November evening when nine great oxcarts with large wooden wheels and bamboo frames, hemp-woven at sides and bottom, slowly made their way along the dirt road that leads to the village of Gurdaspur. They were filled with all the sundry belongings of men that go on pilgrimage. There were bedding for the oxen, cooking vessels, cotton-quilts, grains and flour, hookah pipes and black tobacco, half-dressed children, and jars that hold the holy water of the river. The women rode and many of the men. Those that walked carried on their shoulders, as protection from the *dakus,* their bamboo lathis[1] from which dangled their coarse brown shoes, for why should good leather be worn out unnecessarily? They were rejoicing at their escape from the dangers of the way, and at their safe return, for yonder, less than half a *kos* away, lay their little village.

"Look, brothers, our village has not suffered in our absence. The fields look fair as any we have seen. Mahadev has been compassionate. With offerings of flowers and rice and holy Ganga water shall we rejoice before his sacred *lingam.*"

"See," said another, "our friends have caught sight of us, and are hastening out with drum and cymbal to give us welcome. Now together let us shout, 'Ganga Ji ki jai!' (Praise to great Ganga!), so that they may hear us even at this distance. Chajju, do you lead us; your voice is strong. All together:

"Ganga Ji ki jai! Ganga Ji ki jai!"

The sound rolled out, sharp and clear, over the intervening fields and filled the

[1] Staffs.

"They were rejoicing at their escape from the dangers of the way, and at their safe return"

evening air. The cymbals and the drums in the distance beat out a faint reply.

"Chajju, why did you not join your shout to ours? It is a bad omen. Do you anger the goddess and spoil all the merit of our long pilgrimage? Have we tramped these weary miles that you might undo us at the home-coming?"

"No, my brothers, I meant no harm to you. My heart was heavy. My lips would not frame the name of Ganga. Would you have me shout false praises?"

"This speech is strange from you, Chajju. Have you taken the fever on the way?"

"I have a fever indeed, brothers—a fever of the soul. My heart is burning up. I am parched within, and I shake as a child with ague."

"What is fever that it should stop you in your service of the gods? Ganga will not accept this excuse of yours. Even the dying take the names of the gods."

"Whose name, my brothers, do the gods take when they are dying? Tell me that."

His fellow pilgrims looked one at the other as Chajju spoke; it was some time before any one was bold enough to make reply.

"What words are these, Chajju? You are going mad. Have you the curse of Ganga on you for your sins? Brothers, let us keep our distance from him lest we be smitten too. Alas that we bear home such sorrow! Life is indeed illusion. Our sorrow was joy but a moment ago."

"But a moment ago, did you say? No, my brothers, long ages ago, as we approached the river bank, joy perished in sorrow."

Runners from the welcoming group of villagers were now among the returning pilgrims and questions and answers flew eagerly back and forth. Overhead the great bats flew in solemn array toward the darkness of the eastern sky.

"The news of the village? The daughter of Chiddhu is betrothed to the son of Jumman; Soma has lost his ox; and the mother of Chajju lies sick to death."

A form bounded from the caravan of slow-moving oxcarts, down the road, past the group where drums and cymbals were making their noisy greeting, past the thornbushes in the lane that leads to the village, down the narrow alleys to the right, and into a darkened courtyard surrounded with mud walls. There it stopped. In the room beyond a little wick was burning in mustard oil in an earthen saucer; all else was in shadow. The man outside looked and listened. Some one was moaning piteously within:

"Chajju, my son, may the gods speed thee on thy return. Haste thee, O haste thee, for I am going fast. My hands are weary with this hard holding on to life. It slips through these old and palsied fingers. How many *kos* art thou distant yet? . . . Methought I heard the sound of drums. Is it that he is coming? He is coming with Ganga's blessing. Then shall I fold my hands in peace, and breathe out as a child."

"My mother!"

"Who spoke? It is Mahadev summoning me. O greatest of the gods, call me not forth till I have seen my child. He bears me a necessity for my journey. He will be here briefly. Be pitiful!"

"My mother!"

"O Chajju, is it thy voice, my son, or an illusion of death?"

"Mother, it is I. I would be with thee in this thy last hour. I am here. Let me sit and hold thy hand."

He took her faded, feverish hands in his. She looked into his face with burning eyes, as men look to their deliverer:

"O Chajju, thou art just in time. Mahadev has been calling. He had pity on me and gave me a moment more. Be quick, Chajju! It is but a moment I have. Give me Ganga's blessing; anoint my head and my hands with Ganga's water; pour it down my throat."

"Mother, let us not talk of Ganga now. What is Ganga water at such an hour as this?"

"How strange thy voice sounds, Chajju. The illusion of death is on me. If I had strength to tell thee what I heard thee say, thou wouldst be amazed. Say it again, Chajju, and I will try to hear correctly."

"Mother, what is Ganga water—"

"It is the water of life, my son. Give me it. Do not torment me in my last hour."

"I have none, mother. I thought it not worth the bringing. I have brought something else instead—something I heard."

"What is it, son? The blessing of some other god or goddess? Speak, I am ready for it!"

"No, mother. It is the learning of wise Pandits by the banks of Ganga. They had studied in great schools and they marveled at my ignorance. They taught me what we as Hindus should believe. Ganga and Mahadev are but names, my mother—"

As he spoke he looked at her. She turned her dying eyes on him. Her breast heaved; her breath came short. He could not endure that look of hers, and laid his head upon her arm. The moments passed. After long waiting slowly in the darkness of the room came her faint whisper:

"Chajju, *dakus, dakus!* We have been robbed, my son."

VII

"WHAT'S IN A NAME?"

IT was one of those warm days in South India when the mercury stands around a hundred and twenty in the shade, and you wish there were some shade.

The oxen had toiled through the sand all morning, at the speed of two miles an hour, and as we drew into the little village, they halted in front of the tavern with its three mud walls and a thatched roof, and there they refused to walk another step. It was midday and the sun shone straight down on Talikat Apuram, and I crawled out of the oxcart and into the tavern, feeling very much the same as butter looks in Ohio on a hot July day.

The first thing I observed was a palm-tree pillar and I embraced it like a long-lost friend and then sat on the ground with a feeling of great relief, supporting myself by means of the pillar. I was glad there was a tavern with shade and a floor to sit on and a pillar to hold on to, for it was very, very warm.

There were ten large black men seated on the floor of the tavern, and one of them stepped out for a few minutes and returned with a large jar full of water which he poised above me, and then without asking my permission, poured all over me—and it felt good. Then he went out and got another bucket of water and poured that all over me, and I felt better. Then another and another, and when he had poured the fourth bucket, I surprised that unsuspecting man by starting in to preach.

Brother Shadrach, our Indian preacher, slipped up close to me and nudged me with his elbow, saying, "Iya, they all belong to the robber caste."

Meshach and Abednego have not yet appeared in our Madras District, but Shadrach is a very useful preacher. When he mentioned that they were all Maravars, and hence robbers, I felt very much at home among them. I started telling them the story of the thief on the cross, and how Jesus saved him even there, and told him,

"This day shalt thou be in paradise with me." "You see," I added, "that was a man of your own caste, and Jesus saved him."

Then I told them how Jesus saved me from my sins, and without more preaching I asked them, "How many of you would like to accept this Saviour?" and every man in the room stood up.

It seemed too good to be true, but Shadrach said, "These men are true men and not afraid for anything, and if they set out in this way, they will not turn aside from it."

"Do you understand," I asked, "what dangers lie in the way? Your neighbors will hate you and persecute you for being Christians. Your houses will be burned down, your children beaten on the streets, your women insulted, your lives in great danger all the time."

"All this we know, sir. Twenty-seven years ago an evangelist built a chapel here, and on the night it was dedicated, the Rajah sent his servants to tear it down, and they stabled their horses where the church had stood," was the answer.

"Were there any Christians?" I asked.

"Yes, many, but they were driven out and scattered. Some denied the faith and returned to their idols, and others left the village, for this is the Rajah's village, his own property, and he hated the Christians, and now only one man of that Way remains in our village, an old man, sir."

The name of the village meant many things, and there were strange stories of its origin. It might mean, "The village where heads are displayed," or the "Village that shows its head," or "The village where you dare not show your head," just as you chose to pronounce that ancient name; but the last pronunciation was by far the most common, and bore its own testimony to the character of the little town.

One of the men took from about his neck the rosary of Rudraksha berries sacred to Siva, and handing them over to me, said, "Never will I worship Siva again, henceforth only Jesus Christ." They pleaded with me for baptism, and on Brother Shadrach's advice, I baptized them and took them into the church on probation.

The only other Christian of the village was summoned, and when he heard the news rejoiced beyond measure. For twenty-seven years he had never heard the sound of the gospel, though he had read his Bible and prayed alone in his little house. For fear of persecution he had shut his doors and barred his windows whenever he worshiped God, but the fact that he was a Christian was none the less known to the village. Now he had ten brethren to read and pray with him. Apart from other Christians, he had gone astray in some of his practices, and we had to arrange for his separate maintenance of the second wife whom he had taken when his first proved barren. But he was glad to accede to our requests and proved his eager desire to serve God by every word and act.

Thus was founded the church in Talikat Apuram, "The village where you dare not show your head." When I returned after visiting some other villages, I found thirty new believers who desired baptism and whom we baptized. Then they asked me how they could build a house of worship.

"How much money can you raise to build it?" I asked them.

"Sir, we have no money, and our income is cut off," they answered.

Now, while all Maravars are not robbers, and all, even those that are robbers, are regarded as very respectable by many castes of Hindus, they have regular incomes because they are of the robber caste, and nearly every village has a few families of Maravars whom they gladly support because long experience has taught them that unless they do pay this regular income frequent robberies will deprive the villagers of far more than the cost of that support. And in every case the Maravars of the village, to the last individual, will have a gilt-edged alibi for the entire night of the robbery. But as long as his salary is paid, the Maravar insures the village against robbery of all varieties. However, when he becomes a Christian, the fact that he is no longer a potential robber, or in any sense a menace to the community, is recognized, and the salary is immediately cut off. Thus folks who were comparatively well to do were suddenly forced to seek remunerative employment, and they had no funds to build a church in Talikat Apuram.

In their distress and urgent need of some sort of building which would serve as a place of meeting, they took me to a site on the main street of the town, and there urged me to kneel and pray. This I did, asking God to give them some sort of church, and, as they requested, grant that we might build it on that very plot of ground. Before I left that village, the deed for that piece of land was in my pocket, the donor having made a free gift of it to the Mission for a church building.

But when a week or two had passed, I found a new sign of God's wonderful mercy, for a letter from a little town in southern Ohio brought me news that an old lady there was sending, through the Board of Foreign Missions, eighty dollars to build a little church in India. I fell upon my knees and thanked him for his answer to the prayer of that little congregation of new Christians of the robber caste.

When the little congregation started to build, however, the villagers threatened them with all sorts of trouble, and launched a suit in the neighboring Sub-Magistrate's Court to prevent our work on that land. Unable to secure the injunction they required, they carried the suit to a higher court and there again it was decided in our favor. They appealed again on the ground that the judge, a district munsiff, was a friend of mine, utterly ignoring the fact that he was a Mohammedan. Again, for the third time, the case was decided in our favor, and meanwhile without restriction, the work of building had gone on, until now the tiles were nearly ready to lay and they secured two tile-layers to do the work. These were not Christians, and when the villagers who had found no success by legal means climbed upon the roof with knives and clubs, and threatened to kill them, the tile-layers nearly fell off the roof in their fear and anxiety to get away. It seemed as if the church would never be built in Talikat Apuram.

But at daybreak the following morning the three largest men of our congregation stood out in front of the building with the most blood-thirsty knives they could secure, and with their turbans twisted in warlike guise, and ponderous clubs over their

shoulders, guarded the gate while the tile-layers completed their task on the roof. The mob gathered as before, with clubs and knives, but at sight of those determined faces and huge weapons of destruction, they said, "We declare our neutrality," and faded away. Thus the roof of the little church was tiled at last.

After returning to America, however, I found the best part of the story, for, while visiting in southern Ohio, I called upon the old lady who had built that church, and found that her entire cash income was a pension paid her by the United States government, because her husband had been a soldier in our Civil War, and I asked her how she could build a church with such an income. She answered, "My daughter supplies all my wants and I did not need the money. It all belongs to God, and I merely invested it for him."

After the Church had gained a real influence in the place, I detected a change in the pronunciation of the name of the town, and one day I asked Brother Mathura about it.

"Mathura," said I, "you call your place Talikat Upuram now instead of Apuram. Can you tell me the reason?"

"Sir," he answered, "the nature of the place has changed. Why not the name too? It is now the *village that is showing its head.*"

VIII

ROADS TO PEACE

I WILL tell you the story as he told it to me that day so eventful in both our lives. That was the day on which I discovered his soul and saw it laid bare and throbbing to my brimming eyes. That was the day when he knew I was his friend, when he learned for the first time that I had been watching his career with a solicitude equal to a father's for an ambitious and devoted son. It was the day of our long walk along the barley fields and down the bank of the canal to our distant camp. It all came about by a word of praise cautiously given:

"Your soul was a blazing torch this morning, Tara Chand, and your words were words of fire. The Hindus of the town will have hard work to put out the conflagration you lighted in their hearts."

I feared to say more and waited for his reply. It was long in coming: "Only the heart that burns feels. To be sensitive to sorrow one must know sorrow. To know the Hindu's burden one must have carried it himself, one must still carry it. I am Christian, Padri Sahib,[1] but I am Hindu too. You look strangely at me? It is the Hindu's thirst that I slake at the Christian's fountain; it is the Hindu's burden that I pull with the yoke of Christ. There were two of us—I was the younger—"

He stopped talking as if he had already said too much, and remained silent, rubbing an ear of barley in his hands. Silence is the best of listeners. I was a good listener that morning. Finally he threw away the barley stalks, shrugged his shoulders, and continued:

"It is too long a story—"

"It is a long way to our tents, Tara Chand."

"A long story takes much patience to hear it out, Padri Sahib."

"When it is of friends, patience is an eager listener," I replied.

"You are kind, Padri Sahib—"

---

[1] Title of respect given to a missionary.

He picked up a fallen twig and pulled off the leaves as he spoke, slowly at first:

"There were two of us. I was the younger brother. Our father was dead. My brother took his place. How kind he was to me! We were *halwais* [confectioners] in Sitapur. We were wealthy as Hindus go and had all that we desired. I did not understand my brother, though I thought I knew him. It was he who set my soul on fire—to feel, to suffer, to bear the burden. And yet I knew not till that day that fire consumed his soul. Until that day he kept his burden so concealed that none ever suspected it. That day! That day, Padri Sahib! I count time now from that day. From that day and the other!"

He looked into my face. The fires within his soul were burning uncontrolled:

"I am confusing you. It is hard to tell the thing in order. That day—the day when my brother chose the Hindu's road to peace. The other—when I chose the Christian's road to peace. That day came months before the other, and it is of that day that I shall speak. The other is another story.

. . . He was my brother and I knew him not. He it is that set my soul on fire and keeps it burning. It is the flame of my brother's heart that I passed to others this morning—"

"And to me as well, Tara Chand."

"You are kind, Padri Sahib. What was I speaking of? That day! He had been to a wedding the night before, and in the morning, sitting in the *halwai's* shop together, he began to laugh, and then he said: 'You should have been there last night, Tara Chand. Such feasting and shouting and jesting! You would have thought that the whole city was getting married. There was some drunkenness too, but what of that? One must have merriment.' As he laughed he took up his strainer, and dipping it into the boiling sugar drew out the hot *jalebis*.[1]

"I reached out my hand and lifted one of the sweetmeats. 'Your *jalebis* are good this morning, Din Dayal, my brother,' I said, 'When the heart of the *halwai* is light, his sweets are excellent. You are ever laughing over some escapade, and the laugh goes

[1] An Indian sweetmeat.

into your sugar and flavors it. These wasps and honeybees that settle on your wares tasting their sweetness are related to you, for you, like them, have eye and nose and mouth for the joys of life, and you are ever finding them where freshly made. I wish I were like you.'

" 'I am as the Creator made me, Tara Chand. I love a wedding song and a good *nautch*;[1] I love the clink of jewelry on the ankles of women; I love a dark eye behind a half-drawn veil; I love the stories of Krishna—his sportings with the *Gopis*[2] of Brindaban and his sixteen thousand wives. I love the *Holi* festival with its throwing of colored water, its gambling, and its freedom from restraint. Yet mark you, Tara Chand, all these only on proper occasion. The rest of the time you will find me in my own home or shop as pious as any Hindu householder. And when I fold my hands in prayer before Lord Ganesh—'

"I finished the sentence for him: 'Even Ganesh, the elephant-headed, smiles be-

[1] Dance.

[2] Female cowherds.

tween his tusks; for your smile, my brother, is as contagious as the plague.'

"He stopped me with his raised hand. 'You are dipping your words in sugar this morning, Tara Chand, and warm and fresh they taste good to the soul. But, like a good *halwai* (as you are), leave out the flavor of bitterness. Speak not of the plague! That is a word for Lord Ganesh's ear alone at the *puja* hour. . . . But the wedding, Tara Chand; you should have seen what we did with the bridegroom. I laugh to see him yet.'

"He laughed unrestrainedly, and I laughed too, though I understood not the cause of his merriment. Ram Das, a friend of his, came by, and Din Dayal took up his brass scales and adjusted the strings.

" 'My little brother would hear of the bridegroom, Ram Das, and I cannot stop laughing to tell it. You have a more sober countenance than I. Tell him of the bridegroom, Ram Das, while I weigh you out some *jalebis,* four annas' worth.'

" 'The bridegroom is dead,' said Ram Das.

" 'No, we didn't kill him, Ram Das. Make it out no worse than it was. The truth, the truth, that will make Tara Chand laugh sufficiently.'

" 'The truth, Din Dayal, by the gods I have spoken it. There is no laugh to the truth. They are burning his body now. The screams of the bride—have you not heard them? But I forgot! What can you hear, Din Dayal, surrounded by your sweets? All the world to you is sweets; one large *burfee* wrapped in silver foil. Man, outside your shop there is sorrow! Laugh here all you choose at the bridegroom; yonder we beat our breasts for him.'

"I looked at my brother. He sat as one in a trance, staring vacantly before him, and Ram Das turned to go. I stopped him, trying to excuse my brother. I understood him not, Padri Sahib:

" 'He meant no harm, Ram Das. I am sure he thinks of more than pleasure. He was speaking to me but a moment ago of bitterness. Speak, how came the bridegroom to die?'

"Ram Das turned to me and pointed his

finger at my brother. 'Does he indeed know one word of sorrow? Of bitterness did he speak? Then I tell him, speaking so he may understand. The bridegroom died of —bitterness. I can say no more.'

" 'No, tell us more, Ram Das,' I pleaded, while Din Dayal sat as one unconscious. 'What is bitterness? I bend my ear to you. Stand on your toes and whisper in it!'

"Ram Das reached up his lips and as he spoke in softest tone, my brother laid his head alongside of ours: 'Bitterness? The bubonic plague is bitterness.'

"Ere we had raised our heads Ram Das was gone. It was then I saw for the first time, and even then I understood it not, a look of unutterable sadness steal over the features of my brother. Before I could suspect anything he shook it off with a smile.

" 'Why should you look so solemn, Tara Chand? Let corpses look that! The bride is the widow. You are neither the corpse nor the bride. The bridegroom has had his pleasure and is gone hence. But we are still here. When we have had our pleasure we shall follow him. Just because one of us has ceased from eating and has risen, shall the rest of us call the meal finished and wipe our fingers? Nothing has really changed since yesterday. Sorrow is still sorrow; joy is still joy. *Jalebis,* see, are still sweet—,' and biting into one he held it up between his fingers. 'My little brother, eat that white *pera* next you, all sprinkled with pistachio and cocoanut! There! We feel better. Now let us laugh together!'

"Passers-by wondered at the hearty laughing in the shop of the *halwai.* I myself wondered he could laugh so heartily. He read my looks and answered:

" 'Tara Chand, I laugh because I am wise. No man has better opportunity than the *halwai* to learn true wisdom, as he sits in his shop. Sit here beside me, and let me teach you the true philosophy of life. I am your older brother. Now give attention while I open a mouth of wisdom.'

"He coughed with mock solemnity and I enjoyed hugely his manner.

" 'You see the crowds in the bazaar coming and going, Tara Chand. Let us study them as they pass this shop. There is the rich man in his fine carriage—two servants on the coachman's box, and two standing behind as grooms. There is the Brahman watching his step. There is the villager all eyes and no brains, with legs like a crane

and mouth like an open well. Here is a blind beggar, asking for alms with his monotonous cry. He thinks I can feed all the blind of the city. There is a leper, his nose half gone, his fingers stumps. Here is an orphan—see how his ribs protrude. Sweets are too rich for the starving, therefore I refused him. There is the bold-faced harlot, advertising her trade. The gods pity her victims! Yonder far down the street, headed this way, is a *sadhu* in yellow robe, with his rosary and begging-bowl. He will no doubt reach out for a *luddoo.* These holy men have renounced the world, but not the *halwai's* shop. Their eyes are sharp and their teeth strong for the curds and sugar. And so, my little brother, we sit among the sweetmeats and out yonder the world passes before us, and from this we learn the true wisdom. Be not too tender-hearted. The bazaar is ever filled with people of all sorts. Do not take their affairs to your heart. Look from them to your sweets and to your home behind, but look not too closely at the street where men and women come and go. So shall the joy of life not be given an alms to beggars and diseased.'

"After this merry burst he lapsed into silence. I made no reply, but sat watching the movements of the *sadhu* working his way through the crowd. The minutes passed. Finally my brother heaved a sigh, and taking his scales held them poised. I turned to him and laughed, still unsuspecting, unconscious of the truth.

"'O philosopher of joy, why do you belie yourself with such a groan?'

"He made no reply, and laughing, I repeated the question. Then he spoke and his tone was changed:

"'These scales are accurate and these weights are true. But, alas! Tara Chand, the strings of my heart are all twisted and my wisdom is weighing light. I have given you short weight, little brother, and you, foolish one, have not known it. I have piled on laughter and words, and yet the other scale lifts not. It is very heavy.'

"'What is heavy, Din Dayal? What are you weighing? I do not understand.'

"He remained silent. I was puzzled beyond all measure. When he spoke it was to himself and very slowly:

"'Very strange that Joy mates not with Peace! Again and again have I married Joy as bride to Peace, and Wisdom, as priest, has tied their garments together. Again and again, as now, I have sat down to the wedding feast to enjoy their union.

But the bridegroom—the bridegroom dies of bitterness—'

"A voice broke in upon his meditation:

" 'Peace! the peace of the *sadhu* upon you!'

"Din Dayal raised his eyes. He looked at the *sadhu*. The minutes passed and still he looked. He leaned over his wares and looked more deeply. I reached out my hand to pull him back:

" 'Have a care, Din Dayal! You will fall out of your shop. What do you see that you stare so?'

"My brother still looked at the *sadhu*.

" 'Where did you get it, Holy One?' and his voice trembled as he spoke.

" 'Get what, my brother?' asked the *sadhu*.

" 'Get peace, peace!'

" 'I found it on the road of renunciation.' The *sadhu* spoke the heart of Hinduism.

" 'Is it there for anyone who seeks it?'

" 'It is there, but the road is long and weary. It is a search of many years, and hunger and thirst are fellow pilgrims on the road.'

" 'Can it be found, Holy One? Will there be no disappointment in it?'

" 'It is there if you have the will to reach it. It is certain, sure.'

"My brother turned and looked at me. I never saw that look before and knew not what it meant. He looked at the house behind, where his wife and his little son were sheltered, and then he looked at the *sadhu*.

" 'Holy One,' and he rose as he spoke, 'I follow you on the road of renunciation. Tara Chand, the shop is yours. Go to my child and his mother and give them your best care. Bear them this one message: "Peace is greater than joy!" '

"Ere I could make out what was happening, the *sadhu* and his new disciple disappeared around the corner. When I came to myself I was saying: 'I warned him if he leaned so far he would fall into the road, but I dreamed not of the road of renunciation.' "

He finished the story. I was deeply affected, and began to look for words to comfort him, but Tara Chand interrupted me:

"It is not all the story, Padri Sahib. The

rest is brief, but to me the harder in the telling. If you had come earlier to our city, the tale might have been different. My brother might now be on the other side of you, and this morning two brothers in place of one might have broken the bread of life in the hungry town. You were too late, and he was gone."

I said nothing in reply and he went on:

"Three years ago I saw him once more. It was at the river bank. I was the center of a large crowd. Eager faces looked up to me as I undid the foldings and revealed the meanings of those words which brought me into this way: 'My peace give I unto you. Not as the world giveth, give I.' Padri Sahib, the men of India drink these words as thirsty children. The land you see is parched and brown, but not so parched as the hearts of its people. I had noticed a Hindu sadhu on the edge of the crowd, standing there in all his filth. His body was smeared with cow-dung and streaked with yellow ochre, his face and hair were covered with ashes, his only covering was a loin cloth. He stood at one end and I at

"The men of India drink these words as thirsty children"

the other. There was some space between us. He was not watching me, but staring vacantly before him at the crowd.

"As I spoke, his hard stare—he was a victim of drugs, Padri Sahib—came nearer and nearer. I have felt a strange drawing toward every *sadhu* since that day, and I played for the gaze of this one. I knew not why it was, but I told the story of my brother. The *sadhu* listened unconcerned. It was as though he did not hear. Before I was through with it, a great suspicion flashed upon me. 'Peace is greater than joy,' I shouted and looked hard at him. He lifted his gaze slowly and my eye met his. 'Peace is greater than joy,' I shouted again. I knew him then—it was my brother. He looked at me. He seemed to struggle with his memory, as if trying, in great weakness, to recollect some incident long forgotten. All in vain. He lapsed into that vacant stare.

"I rushed through the crowd to him. They wondering at my action. 'Din Dayal, *halwai* of Sitapur! I am your brother, Tara Chand.' The man was drugged and heard not. Passionately I seized him by the arm. 'We have both been seekers after peace, my brother. Speak, Din Dayal, if you understand me now!'

" 'The Holy One hears you not,' said a bystander; 'his thoughts are far from here.'

"As I stood looking at him the voices out of the crowd became ever more insistent: 'Come, tell us more of a peace such as the world gives not.'

"I yielded to them. . . . I never saw my brother again!"

"That was a test indeed, Tara Chand. Did the peace that you had found stand the strain?" I asked.

"That is why I speak to-day as I do, Padri Sahib." He smiled and pointed ahead.

"Here are the tents, and the end of my long story."

IX

THE LAWYER-PREACHER

ONE day a big, broad-shouldered lawyer of my congregation came to see me, and with one of those beautiful Oriental smiles, said, "Missionary, I want to be a preacher."

"Vetha Nayagam," said I, "aren't you making by the practice of law three or four times as much as any of my preachers ever make?"

"Yes," he answered.

"Then why do you want to preach? Besides," I added, "I cannot pay you even what I am paying my other preachers. I can pay you nothing at all."

"Sir," he asked, "have I asked you for any money?"

"No," I answered, "but you have a wife and children to support, and you cannot work without any salary."

"Missionary," was the reply, "if you will

just give me permission to preach, I will sell my property back in Sinnia Puram and live on the proceeds as long as anything remains, and when that is all gone, perhaps I shall have gathered from among the heathen a congregation which will at least be able to support my family and me, and if not, you have many rich people in America who could easily do that."

I was delighted, and with great pleasure wrote him out an exhorter's license, signifying that D. Vetha Nayagam was hereby licensed to preach the gospel in Sinnia Puram and the surrounding villages. We knelt down together and thanked God for giving us this new preacher, and he set out at once for his village. Before he reached home his house was burned down over the heads of his wife and three little children. Persecution is a very common means of preventing the gospel reaching the poor and downtrodden. I have had many of my poorest parishioners come to me with great bleeding gashes across their backs, and more than a hundred of their houses burned down for the one crime of becoming Christians.

So when I heard of another house burned down I just went as soon as I could to his village and found Vetha Nayagam and his family in that ruin of a house. They had spread a few shocks of grain over the charred remains of the rafters, so there were a few spots within the walls where one could sit down without getting sunstroke under that blazing sun. After talking with them all for a few minutes I suggested that it would be well for us to pray, and we all knelt down together, Vetha Nayagam, his wife, and the three children—Paul Stephen, aged ten; Grace, aged eight; and little Arthur Theophilus, aged six. I wish you could have heard that tiny fellow sing the one hundred and thirty-third Psalm in Tamil, "Behold how good and pleasant it is for brethren to dwell together in harmony." India sadly lacks the harmony.

Of course I prayed first, because God listens first to white people. Don't you believe that? Well, haven't we always acted as if he did? I said: "O God, this man has lost his house because he started in to preach thy gospel. Please give him another house, for Jesus' sake. Amen." When I had finished I felt as if I had really prayed a great prayer, but I remembered and said, "O Vetha Nayagam, will you pray?"

He prayed: "O God, I have not asked this missionary for any salary, and I do not want pay in money, but give me for my salary the hearts of all the people around here, that I may bring them into thy kingdom, for Jesus' sake. Amen."

Now when I heard Brother Vetha Nayagam's prayer it seemed to me that the big petition I had just asked of God was about the size of little Arthur Theophilus, and that was the way I felt too, alongside my Indian brother, but over in the corner of the house his little brown wife was kneeling, and she looked so neat and nice and the children were so sweet and clean, that I felt sure she could pray too, and so I asked her, "Sister, will you pray?"

"O Father," she pleaded, "please forgive the people who burned our house down. Forgive them and save them, and bring them into thy kingdom, for Jesus' sake. Amen."

In that one year Vetha Nayagam brought three hundred and sixty people into the kingdom of God. Three hundred and sixty people are worth more than the finest house that ever was built. Pray for your enemies? Why, of course! That was what Jesus commanded us to do. It is worth while praying for your enemies when you realize that you secure results like that.

In every village to which he went, people sought the Lord and begged me to come out and baptize them. I had just baptized a hundred or more in the village of Kumara Puram, and the next morning was sitting in the village telling the people about America. They have gotten Christ mixed up with America in their minds and seem to think they are connected in some way. I wish we thought so more here in America! So whenever I tell them about Christ, they want to hear about America.

A good number of them sat around me on the ground listening to my stories, when there came across the village an old man, all doubled up and leaning upon his staff, crawling rather than walking. He would have been quite tall had he stood erect, but looked as if he never had stood erect. You never saw anyone so hungry-looking in all your life, yet he was only one of the fifty million Indian people always on the verge of starvation. Behind him walked ten or twelve younger men, but not one of them would walk in front of the old man; that would not be respectful, and heathen India knows how to respect old men.

Before I dreamed of his purpose he fell at my feet and clasped them in his bony arms and said, "Missionary, will you read our petition?"

I took him by his bony old shoulders and lifted him from the ground and seated him upon the old wooden mortar that served me as a seat. Then I said: "Never do that to me any more. I am just a man like you. Where is your petition, Old Man?" "Old Man" is the most respectful title you can use in addressing people in South India.

Out of his loin-cloth, his only garment, he took a great sheet of paper and handed it over to me, saying, "You will have to read it. We do not know how to read."

Written in Tamil, it read like this: "Reverend and Dear Sir, we the undersigned, a hundred and sixty-five people of Nagalapuram Village, desiring to become Christians, present this petition begging you to come to our village and baptize us. We have thrown away our old gods and will never worship them any more. We have heard of your God and want to serve him, and to show you that we are in earnest we have all signed our names to this petition."

Sign their names! There was not one of them that could have read his name had he seen it signed. Do you know how they signed their names? In every large village there lives a professional letter-writer and Nagalapuram is a town of ten thousand people, so they got the letter-writer to write out the whole petition and then every one of them put his thumb-impression in ink on the back of that petition, and the scribe wrote the name of each individual after the thumb-impression. There they were, a hundred and sixty-five of them.

Talk about your authentic documents! Why, somebody might forge your signature to-morrow, but nobody could ever forge your thumb-impression. There aren't two alike in the whole wide world.

So I took the petition and said to the old man, "Kattayan, I am glad you wish to be a Christian, and that the villagers want to come to Christ, but I cannot give you a pastor, and until you have a pastor, I cannot baptize you, for you do not know how to lead a Christian life."

"Sir, they may kill us, if they will, but whether we live or die, we will surely be Christians."

"Kattayan," said I, "I know you could die for Christ, but you do not know how to live for him. Till you have instruction you cannot be baptized."

"Sir," he pleaded, "I am a very old man. All these years I have waited and now you have come. I may never see you again. Please baptize me, so that when I die I can go to God and tell him I am a Christian."

"Did you have cholera in the village last year?" I asked.

"Yes, sir, three hundred and seventy-two people died in one month, with cholera."

"Will it come back this year?"

"Sir," he answered, "it comes every year."

"Suppose," said I, "we baptized you and when the cholera came, your own boy should lie dying of cholera and should ask you to pray for him, what would you do, Old Man?"

"Sir," he cried, "I do not know what I should do."

"You would go down to the creek," said I, "where your old gods were thrown into the mud, and digging one of them out, you would call on your old god to save your son."

"That is right. That is what we would do," he said.

"You see," I said, "you do not know how to be Christians until we can send you a pastor who will show you how to pray to the living God who can hear and answer your prayers."

"That is true. Give us a preacher, give us a preacher!"

"But," I objected, "can you support a preacher if I send you one? How much money could you give him a month?"

"Sir," he pleaded, "we never get money, but we will give him some of our millets, ragi, cholam, kumbu."

"O, I cannot send a man there without something better than that."

"But, sir, that is all we have, and we are very poor." There was no need to mention their want. I could count every bone of his poor old body.

"Old Man," said I, "I will try to get some friends of mine to help support your preacher, and I will send you one as soon as I can. Now, do not cry, but go back to your village and I will tell my friends about your desire to be Christians, and they will help you."

And I sent the old man and his followers back to Nagalapuram, but I translated their petition and sent copies of it to many friends and asked them to take the support of a native preacher for Nagalapuram at fifty dollars a year together with what Kattayan and his people would pay toward his support.

A year passed and I found myself avoiding Nagalapuram, and because I had not gotten them a preacher; but thus far no one answered my letters. They just concluded that I was a beggar, and paid no attention to my pleas. Another year hastened away after the first, and still no answer—no preacher. Then I sent Raju to visit the village and his postcard spoke thus, "Dear Brother Kingham: To-day I am in Nagalapuram as you instructed me. Old Kattayan is dying, and said I should tell you he wants you to come and baptize him, so he can go to God and tell him that he is a Christian."

It was the rainy season and oxcarts could not be had for love or money, for all the oxen were plowing, so I walked. It was fifty miles to walk and the Vaippar was in flood, but one night at midnight I found myself in Nagalapuram, and hunted among the houses of ten thousand people till I found the little mud-walled, thatch-roofed house of old Kattayan. There by the flickering light of a cocoanut oil lamp, I baptized the old man in the name of the Father and of the Son and of the Holy Ghost.

I had hardly finished his baptism when

people crowded around me there and in the street saying: "Baptize me, baptize me. I too wish to be a Christian. I have been waiting two years. Here is this little boy. He has waited two years."

Perhaps you would have had more determination than I had, for between midnight and morning I baptized every one whose name was on that petition, a hundred and sixty-five. I felt it was not right to keep them waiting longer.

Then they gathered around me again and said, "That preacher—have you got us that preacher?"

"No," I said, "I could not get him. I have no money for him."

"But you said you would write to America."

"I did write letters to my friends in America."

"Did you tell them we wanted a preacher?"

"Yes," said I.

"Did you tell them we were poor?" they asked.

"Yes, I told them you were poor," I said.

There was a long interval of silence, and then some one said, "Say, did you mail those letters?"

I could stand it no longer, and so, bidding them farewell, I came away, and for the next two years I still avoided Nagalapuram. For still I waited in vain for the answer to my request for a preacher for that village.

Then one day a brother of Vetha Nayagam, the lawyer-preacher, came to see me and said, "Sir, I too desire to be a preacher."

Knowing his knowledge of the Scripture and his general ability, I said, "Do you know the salary I am paying your brother, Vetha Nayagam?"

"Yes," he said, "I know."

"Will you take the same pay?" I asked.

"Yes, sir," was his glad response, and I appointed him as pastor of a hundred and sixty-five probationers in Nagalapuram village on a salary of "nothing a month and board yourself," and sell what you have to support yourself while you preach the gospel. He was delighted to get it.

As soon as they had a pastor there, I went to Nagalapuram. As I drew near I saw the people coming out to meet me, and who do you suppose was the very first in the procession?

You remember old Kattayan, who was dying? Well, after he was baptized and received into the church on probation he did not die. He got well, and it was he who came hobbling along on his old staff and got my hand into that bony hand of his, and shook and shook and shook. He was a sort of natural born Methodist.

"What's the matter?" I asked.

"Matter?" said he. "Didn't you know we had a preacher?"

"Is he any good?" I asked.

"Sir," he answered, "we never did have such a preacher." This was quite true. They did not have a man, woman, or child who could read a verse out of the Bible in their own Tamil tongue. They did not have a Sunday school teacher, nor an Epworth League officer, nor even a Ladies' Aid Society, and yet for four years in the face of a hostile and persecuting heathen-

In an ancient stronghold of Hinduism

ism, they had stood firm and had not backslidden.

"Well, I am glad you like your preacher," I ventured.

"Yes, sir," was the answer, "he has started a school, and our boys and girls are learning to read and write, and my boy can say a number of verses out of the Bible, and I too have learned some Bible verses and can recite them," and if I had not headed him off, Kattayan would have rattled off every verse he knew.

"I am glad you like your preacher," I repeated.

"Yes," he said; "now we want a church."

"But, Kattayan, have you any money to build a church?"

"No, we haven't any money, but that preacher you gave us told us if there was anything we wanted we should just ask God for it, and we thought we could get you to just tell him that we want a church."

Kattayan took me by the hand and showed me the way up a back alley and around a corner to an old cowshed. What use any member of that congregation ever had for a cowshed I do not know, but I am sure that none of them had ever owned a cow. Perhaps the grandfather of one of them had. At any rate, there was the cowshed.

"What is this?" I asked.

"Missionary, this is where we hold services."

There was room for twenty-five inside and for a hundred and forty outside, so the whole congregation was accommodated. Some of us got inside, and as they had asked me to pray, I prayed as follows: "O God, these people have been starved all their lives, and are hungry even now. They have no money to build a church, but they want a church. O God, please give them some kind of a church, for Jesus' sake. Amen."

Kattayan then took me out on the main street of the town and showed me a little plot of ground. "There," he said, "is where we are going to build that church."

"But," I said, "hadn't you better wait till you get some money before you talk of building?"

"Money?" said he. "Money? Say, didn't you just ask God for that church?"

"Kattayan," said I, "excuse me—I have —urgent business in Tuticorin. I must go. Salaam." And I left the village.

Do you know why I went away so hurriedly? I can tell you the reason. When your missionary finds that some of his new converts out of heathenism have more faith in the living God than the missionary, that is a good time for the missionary to move. So I moved.

I went back to Tuticorin, and when I got there found a letter waiting upon my table—a letter from a little town in Kansas of which I had never heard and signed by a lady whose name I did not know. It read thus:

"Dear Brother Kingham: Dr. Schermerhorn was preaching in our church last night and said that you needed a lot of little churches in your villages in India, and that the natives could put up quite a church building if they had fifty dollars help. My father was going to give me a diamond ring, but I told him, 'Father, I don't want the ring, just give me the money and I will send it out to Brother Kingham to build a church.' So here it is. Please build the best church you can with this fifty dollars, and when it is finished send me a picture of it. This building is to be a memorial to my little sister who died when she was five."

How many of the folks who are listening to this letter believe that the Almighty God who swings the planets in their orbits and keeps the seventy-year meteors on time to the second, would listen to the prayer of a group of poor, half-starved, half-naked, ignorant black people praying in an old cowshed under that blazing sun in South India, and do what they asked of him? Do you suppose he would listen to their prayer? Why, of course he did. And he heard it, as he promised, even before it was uttered. That is what God promises in his Word to do.

I gave the money to Samuel and told him to go ahead and build that church, and he did. Every member of that little congregation—men, women, and children—helped. They managed to get a holiday from their taskmasters, and the walls went up rapidly.

One day Samuel, the pastor, was up on the walls supervising and helping in the work when three men came that way and called him, "Hey you, fellow, come here. We want no church in this village."

"Well, men," he answered, "what are you going to do about it?"

"If you go on building that church, you will die a sudden, horrible, and violent death," they threatened, their black faces still blacker with hatred.

"Men," said he, "I am building that little church for Jesus Christ, and I am not afraid of anything you can do to me."

And with a smile, he said, "Salaam," and returned to his work. The church was completed in a few days.

Then he sent me a note, "Please come over and help us celebrate. The church building is completed."

It was one of the darkest nights I ever traveled, and I walked only five miles, but over the roughest, rockiest road imaginable, and when I got to the church the whole congregation was out in front; and as soon as I arrived they formed a procession, the men carrying torches and the women and children joining in the singing with the men leading and the band in front. Such a band! You never saw such a band. You never heard such a band. And you would not want to hear it again if you did hear it. And last of all they brought me, seated ten feet above the heads of the admiring throng in a wedding car, the kind you ride around in the day you get married down there in South India. And we went around the town, up one street and down another, the band ahead, the people marching and singing, and the wedding car in the rear, pulled by two oxen, while the voices of our Christians rang out in their favorite song:

> "The Lord is my shepherd. I shall not want.
> He maketh me to lie down in green pastures."

And while they sang there were many who were hungry, many who had not had one good square meal for years, if ever!

Up in my exalted seat I found my heart overflowing with joy for the light that was beginning to shine after all these centuries of idolatry. When the procession was over we returned to the little church and knelt there to thank God for his love in giving us at last a preacher and a church.

Then Samuel said, "It is very late. Let me show you where you are to spend the night," and took me to a little stone building in a corner of the town, gave me a cot, and left me to go to the little Hindu restaurant where he always had his meals.

It was very late, but he had forgotten all about supper until then. While he was eating his food he collapsed there on the floor of the little restaurant, for some one had given him with his food enough arsenic to kill five men.

He did not die that night. It was too big a dose, and he did not die till the third day, and then in excruciating agony.

Not dreaming of his danger I called his brother, the lawyer-preacher, Vetha Nayagam, to come with me to Kottur, where we had people to baptize. He did not return to the village till the third day, just in time to see Samuel's horrible and violent death.

The fifth day, returning from Tuticorin, I met him on the road and got out of my oxcart to meet him. His great chest was heaving and his eyes were full of tears.

"What is the matter?" I asked.

"Pastor, they have murdered my brother," and he told me of the threat and the whole story.

As I remembered what he had undergone, my blood boiled.

"What is the use of your preaching?" I asked. "You gave up your law business at which you were making money. You labored a long time without any pay, and even now are receiving but a little help from the mission. On the day you started in to preach, your house was burned down over the heads of your family, and now—now they have murdered your brother. They would rather have murdered you, because you have the larger congregation. You had better give up preaching. Give it up and go back to your law business. You have had to sell nearly everything you had in order to preach thus far, and you still have a wife and children to support."

As I looked I saw that through his tears Vetha Nayagam was smiling at me, as he answered, "Pastor, my brother was a saint of the Living God, and to-day he is a martyr to Jesus Christ; and if God should give me the privilege of dying such a death as he died, I should praise his name forever."

X

WHEN OUTCASTES DREAM

JIWAN DAS sat in the door of his little mud hut at the evening hour. He held in his hand the stem of his *hookah,* but he was not thinking of the flavor of the black tobacco mixed with *gur*. He was not thinking even of his own great weariness, though he had been that day to a distant village. His eyes were on the red glow of the western sky, fading as quickly as the red of the glowing embers in his pipe-bowl. The children and the goats as they passed in and out of the doorway almost stumbled over him, but Jiwan Das paid no heed. He was in deep thought—an unusual state for any simple villager of North India,—or any other part of the land!

"The dream," he finally whispered to himself, "the dream. What means the dream?"

"The dream again!" snapped a woman's voice within. "Shall we never be rid of the dream? Thy children are starving, thy cattle grow daily less fit for work, thy neighbors laugh openly at thy madness. Who knows whither thou art wandering day by day? Why not tell the dream and be done with it?"

Jiwan Das arose, tall and so thin that if any was starving you might say it was he. His little son was playing on the ground before him, planting broken *genda* flowers in the dirt. The father picked him up with a laugh.

"Ah, we shall lift thee high, my boy, if our dream lies not. The dream, portion of my heart, the dream will make thee great. Thou wilt live in a great house with many servants and walk in gardens where more than *gendas* grow. Then wilt thou look down on thy old father, the Chamar, and laugh at him, even as thou art doing now." Jiwan Das shouted in exhultation.

"Listen to the outcaste," laughed the voice within, a bitter laugh. "One would think he was a Brahman trained at Kashi to hear him talk. Thy son, man, will walk his lifelong behind the buffaloes; twisting their tails and thwacking their backbones with his bamboo staff. Such is *my* dream for him, the dream of a woman who knows."

The father drew the son to his heart, and whispered low: "Child, the dream is our secret. It will make thee great. 'Tis not for ears of women. It is for *men,* and thou shalt hear it."

He walked to the end of the courtyard, and into the ear of his infant son whispered long and low. Could you but have seen the face that moment of our villager and the smile of the three-year-old as though he understood!

The next afternoon it was the little daughter that was troubled.

"Mother, where does our father go, leaving the field and the boy to you and me? Where is he now?"

"Thy father, Parbati, is mad. Some evil spirit has possessed him. I have already given of my jewelry to the priest to rid him of the demon. He comes this very day, he has promised me, with powerful *mantras*[1] to speak over him. You must help

[1] Incantations.

me ere he comes to lay out the offerings. The gods are angry and so we starve."

"But, mother, our father seems so sure—"

"So mad! Hush, *laundia!*"[1]

Jiwan Das strode suddenly into the courtyard. He brought with him a stranger.

"Be pleased to sit upon this cot. I will call my brothers. You shall speak to all of us. Your words will melt our hearts. It is an assurance of my dream."

But the crowd had gathered already, wondering who the man might be.

"He is no Hindu of these parts, for he wears a beard. He is no Moslem either: see his Hindu cap! What can he be?"

"See you not his books that he is drawing from his bag? He is some learned Pandit. Knows he not we are Chamars?"

"His face is kindly, brothers. Let us hear him, sitting here, for he makes signs to speak to us."

The stranger had risen, and the simple crowd bent forward to catch his every word.

"I will sing you a song of the new age, a song of Ishwar's new incarnation, a song

[1] Girl.

of great salvation, a song which men now sing through all of Hindustan. Would you hear it?"

"Sing it," said they, "we listen."

And the stranger sang:

"Jai, Prabhu Yishu, jai adhiraja,
Jai, Prabhu, jai jaikari.

"Pap nimit dukh laj uthai,
Pran diyo balihari.

"Tin dinon taba Yishu gora men
Tija diwasa nihari."

"Praise to Lord Yishu (Jesus); praise to the great King.
Praise to the Lord; praise and rejoicings."

"For sin he suffered pain and shame.
His life he gave an offering.

"Three days he lay within the grave.
The third day he was seen again."

"But what means the song? I will now explain it to you—" He was interrupted by a voice:

"Munshiji, is there in your song nothing of making our children great? They walk behind the oxen now; may they not ride behind them? From birth they are taught to fear; may they not learn to be unafraid? Honor is for Brahmans and high-caste men. Is there not for the son of the outcaste some share of wisdom and of wealth? Is it not so in your book there? I have dreamed—"

The stranger paused a moment, then opened the book:

"Your dream is true. There is such a word written here. The great Avatar of Ishwar, by name Yishu, took the children of certain lowly in his arms and he said: 'Let these little children come unto me, and do not hold them back, for to such as these belongs the *Raj* of Ishwar.' "

"Good," said the voice. "Now tell us what the *Raj* may be over which our children are to rule, if we become devotees of Yishu. Let us hear him, brothers. It is a great word. I have heard it already in my dream."

And the stranger began: "It is not to men alone, but to women, and even to little children that this good news comes. It is written here," and he laid his finger on the opened page, "that in this Yishu when we take his sign upon us and name his name, it is as though we were awakened from long sleep. The night is passed away, the day is come. And in the light of this new day our children are to grow, to learn, to become great. I was born such as you. The name of Yishu has made me what I am—"

Jiwan Das could restrain himself no longer. He rose in all his height.

"We be simple people, Munshiji. We know less than babes. We are slow to comprehend; we understand only in pictures. There is much we can never know. We hold together, living in the great *biradari* of our caste. It is hard to change our ways, the customs of our fathers. But your words are pulling us. They are as the sun breaking through the rain-clouds. Send us then a teacher and we will learn." He hesitated, then spoke again more slowly: "As for me, I am ready. Give me the sign of Yishu."

Till then no one had noticed the silent figure in the doorway with close-drawn *chadar,* her hand pressing hard upon her beating heart. Parbati, holding her brother on her hip, clung to the woman's skirts. Only now, when Jiwan Das had spoken, did they see her standing there, did they hear her scream, as if the evil demon had passed to her. They watched her beat her breasts and tear her hair. They saw her beyond all control. They heard the frantic cries of her frightened children.

Jiwan Das stood staring at the door of his own home.

"The dream said nothing of this. It was not in the dream. O Munshiji, what is there in those books of thine that tells of *this?*"

The stranger hastily leafed the pages and ran his eye up and down the columns:

"It is here. I have it now—the words of Yishu," and he traced the passage with his finger as he read, "Think not that I came to send—"

He was interrupted by a solemn, sepulchral voice, speaking slowly, sonorously, threateningly from beyond the entrance of the courtyard:

"Am ...... Hrim ...... Krim ...... Shrim ...... Swaha......"

Jiwan Das and the stranger turned.

There at a distance stood the old Brahman priest pouring out *mantras*, incantations, magic words, a stream of them. The crowd scattered as sheep before the wolf. Who would be caught in those sacred syllables or those fierce curses?

Now was the soul of Jiwan Das hard beset. The simple villager stood transfixed with fear. The words of incantation fell heavy upon him, and he reeled beneath their weight.

"O Munshiji, quick, quick! Knowest thou no *mantras* from thy book?"

The stranger was quick to respond, and he joined his voice to the confusion, speaking distinctly:

"The Injil[1] is greater than the Vedas. Listen to the *mantras* of the Injil. They protect the Chamar from the Brahman. 'All authority hath been given unto me, and lo I am with you alway. . . . And ye shall be hated of all men for my name's sake, but he that endureth to the end he shall be saved. . . . And all things whatsoever ye shall ask in prayer believing ye shall receive.' Jiwan

[1] The Gospel.

Das, let us ask: On that side, O Yishu, thou hearest the screams of his wife and children; on this side the incantations of his priest. They bear him down. In the power of the Injil, for the sake of his boy and the fulfillment of his dream, now hold him fast!"

Jiwan Das smiled faintly, as victors smile after hard struggle.

"It is enough. I shall name the name of Yishu in the hearing of the boy."

That night they brought him to his home unconscious and talking wildly. His neighbors had waylaid him on his way back from a distant village, whither he had escorted the stranger home.

"Seeing the *mantras* have failed, let us see what a bamboo *lathi* can do in driving out evil spirits." They had made the test in the sugar cane fields and were watching the results.

"Fear not. It takes hard hitting to drive out such spirits as possessed him," said one, sitting by his bedside. "They go not out by gentle strokes—"

"He seems to talk more sensibly thus than

when he is awake," said another. "The beating is already doing good. See, he speaks of gods and priests."

"Rejoice, woman! He is calling for a priest. Thy man is better. Quick! Have the priest here! He is coming to his senses now. 'Twas the right remedy."

"Priest! Priest! the Brahman Priest!" moaned the wounded man.

"The priest is here, Jiwan Das. Speak! He can hear thee from his distance."

Jiwan Das raised himself—his eyes were blazing:

"Priest! Brahman Priest! My dream concerns thee. Thou hast heard of my dream? Woulds't know it? Thou shalt hear it. I am not afraid to tell it to thee. It is more powerful than thy mantras upon me. Listen."

He was sitting bolt upright and breathing hard.

"Thy son, Priest, committed murder. He was brought to trial. The Judge sat in his court. The Judge pronounced sentence upon thy son. It was a heavy sentence. And the Judge? Who was *he?* Ha! The

Judge? Yea, the Judge? . . . The Judge was low-born, an outcaste. . . . The Judge was Chamar. . . . Thy son was Brahman. . . . The Judge was Christian. So I saw it in my dream. . . . The Judge was wealthy. The Judge was learned. The Judge was just. . . . The Judge was . . . the Judge, O Priest, was . . . *my son!*"

He fell back exhausted. Men covered their eyes and shook with the terror of the moment. Jiwan Das faintly but distinctly took up his own words:

"Let it be so. I am ready. Give me the sign of Yishu."

XI

IN HIS BLINDNESS

THEY were repairing the bridge over the Ganges Canal on the main high-road and it was with great impatience that I made the long detour. It was noon and I was hot, tired, and dusty, for I had ridden twenty miles that morning on my bicycle, and had preached in three villages where there were Christians. Here was a shady mango grove beside the road. Its challenge to stop and declare oneself its friend could not be resisted. Walking well into its shady depths, I leaned my bicycle against one tree and myself against another. My lunch was good. I had laid my head upon the book I carried with me and was just falling off into sleep when I heard a dull tap-tap-tap at no great distance. I turned my head and saw a blind man coming through the grove, his bamboo staff hitting the ground before him as he walked. Blind men are such common sights in India that I determined to let him pass without a word. He was evidently from the little village that lay half a mile behind the grove. I watched him as he came slowly on. He was an old man with long, white beard. There was an air of respectability about him. He was well dressed, wearing *kurta, pajama,* and *pagri,* an unusual combination for a blind man in a village. He was evidently no beggar. I began to be interested. As he drew nearer I noticed that each tap of his *lathi* was accompanied by an ejaculation. I soon detected what it was:

"Ai hamare Bap! Ai hamare Bap!" ("Our Father! Our Father!") I wondered at it. "I have never heard that expression used before," thought I. "It is a queer colloquialism."

Through the trees came the taps and the strange words and the blind man drew very near:

"Ai hamare Bap! Ai hamare Bap! Ai hamare Bap!"

I had not noticed that my bicycle lay in his path. He ran his staff against it, and it fell over with a loud noise. The old man stopped—terrified:

"Ai hamare Bap jo asman par hai" ("Our Father who art in heaven"), fell from his trembling lips.

I sat up as if struck a blow.

The old man was kneeling beside the bicycle, his hands folded, his sightless eyes lifted as he prayed:

"Hamare qusuron ko muaf kar." ("Forgive us our trespasses.")

Something held me still silent. I watched him closely. He did not know what he had done or how to repair the damage. Perplexity covered his features. His staff lay on the ground. His hands groped over the wheels, the frame, the saddle.

"What is it?" he pleaded, as if some one stood at his elbow. "Ai hamare Bap, what is it? I am old, I am blind, I am an ignorant villager—how should I know what to do with it?"

My heart was overflowing with pity and I opened my mouth to speak. But his words forced me back to silence.

"Can it be? Can it be? Is it the An-

"'What is it?' he pleaded, as if some one stood at his elbow"

swer? After all these years is this the Answer? At last the Answer? God be praised!" His face was lighted up: "For forty years I have been hungry, O so hungry! And every morning and every night I have prayed 'Hamari rozina ki roti aj hamen baksh de' ["Give us this day our daily bread"], bread to satisfy the hunger here," and he laid his withered trembling hand on his heart. "Is this the Answer? Does this bring the bread? Surely this is the handiwork of God!" His hands were fingering the spokes. "No man could ever make this. I have found the Answer." And stooping low he laid his forehead reverently upon the pedal and held the dusty chain in both his hands.

His whole attitude was expectant, as if he were sure he had received the gift and yet understood it not. He needed some explanation of it. He was as Moses who saw the bush burning unconsumed, but as yet had heard no words that told him what it meant.

I leaped to my feet. He heard the noise and turned his sightless eyes to me. Blind they were, but not without expression. I could see behind their drawn veils the fierce struggle for vision. He knew not what stood before him—God or angel or man. He would compel his eyes to tell him.

Softly and slowly I spoke:

"Bare Mian,[1] your prayer is heard. I am sent with bread for thee. Sit up and I will share it with thee."

He sat up. "You have brought the bread"—and he reached out both hands (hands covered with grease and grime) as if to receive it—

"Not for your hands, Bare Mian, but for your heart! It is not bread of earth, but bread come down from heaven."

"I know it. I was as a silly child. In my joy I forgot for the moment. But it is You who 'forgives us our trespasses.' "

"It is not I who forgives, Bare Mian."

The look of perplexity again stole over his face.

"I know not what to call you."

I hesitated, fearing a rude shock to his simple faith. "Bare Mian, call me Padri

[1] A title of respect, pronounced Burray Meeah.

Sahib. I am a missionary whom our heavenly Father has sent this way."

He caught at the word and his blind face broke into a smile. "It is the Answer! Padri Sahib! It was a Padri Sahib who forty years ago taught me the Lord's Prayer, and put the water on my head—here! That was in the days when I could see. I came back to my village and I lost my sight. I have been unable to find him since, though I go nearly every day through this grove and sit beside the road, hoping he or some other Padri Sahib may pass this way and speak to me sitting there. The villagers laugh at me, thinking me very silly. The passers-by think I am come to beg, and drop their alms beside me. All this I can endure—their laughter and their pity—if in the end, before I die, I hear a Padri Sahib's voice."

He paused a minute. "You are not my Padri Sahib. A blind man's ear is sharp. But you are his son whom he has sent in his stead."

I hesitated—"What was his name, Bare Mian?" I asked him, timidly.

He named a name.

"I am his son; you have said right. In truth I am," I answered, proudly.

The old man laid his forehead on his folded hands. "The answer to the blind man's prayer is complete. 'Thine is the kingdom, and the power, and the glory.'" He lifted his head again. "And now for the bread, Padri Sahib."

That grassy spot beside the Sea of Galiliee is found in all the world and men still feed the hungry there; the well of Samaria springs forth even in distant mango groves and there men give to those that ask for living water. But such privilege of service is reserved for those whom the King delights to honor. For three long hours I was the honored one that day.

"Look, Bare Mian" (I had forgotten I was dealing with a blind man), "the sun is half down the heaven. I have been long with you. I have here bread that I must break to-night to other hungry ones. They will have waited hours when I reach them. I must go."

"Hours, Padri Sahib? What are *hours?*

I have waited forty *years*. Let them wait. They will be the hungrier and eat more heartily. I am not yet filled—so great was my emptiness."

I rose to go. "Bare Mian, one must not let little children suffer for want of bread. These I go to are little ones, Christians only a year, and faint from hunger."

He took the end of his beard in his hand and held it up trembling. "Padri Sahib, let not this white beard of mine deceive you. I too am nothing but a child."

"I have many children," I said, "and I must feed them all. Some are very small, smaller, than you. You can walk, Bare Mian; for forty years you have kept from falling."

"True, Padri Sahib. I totter along with my two staffs in the two darknesses, one for each darkness. I am doubly blind, you know."

"I do not understand."

"You see it is like this, Padri Sahib. In the one darkness I tap-tap along with a bamboo staff; in the other I tap-tap along with the Lord's Prayer, which is all I know.

With my staffs I am ever sounding out the ways of life."

"Remember what I have told you to-day, Bare Mian. That will give you light along your path when I am gone. I have many others—"

"When you are gone? Many others? Are they blind and neglected and left exposed to die as I am? There is a story—how often I have tried to tell it to others, but I have forgotten its ending, Padri Sahib. My neighbors are ever asking me if I remember it. It is of a lamb that was lost in the darkness, and the man whose lamb it was left his many others. That is as far as I get with it. Tell me, Padri Sahib, was the lamb in the darkness found? Did the man whose lamb it was feed it and leave it there, saying he had other lambs to feed and could not stay longer? Did the lamb in the darkness bleat after him when he was gone? Tell me the story, Padri Sahib."

It was hard to get away from him. I sat down again. "Listen, Bare Mian, I will tell you the story and then I must go. It is getting night."

"Was the man whose lamb it was afraid of the night? Was it only the little lamb that grew accustomed to darkness?"

"Bare Mian, you do not understand. You see this is an out of-the-way village—"

"Was the little lamb lost on the high-road then, Padri Sahib, in a place easy to find? Why, then, was it lost so long? But I have forgotten the story and sit here silently to hear it told once more."

I told the simple story and the tears rolled down the blind man's face. When I came to the shepherd lifting the lamb on his shoulder he broke into sobs and stopped me, exclaiming—

"The lamb was found and lifted from the darkness! For forty years sitting by the roadside I have prayed that that might be the ending of the story. So the lamb was really lifted from the darkness! It is enough!"

His heart was full. He had all he could contain. I waited for his word to go on. Ere it came a look of horror overspread his face:

"The shepherd did not set him down

again, did he? Tell me it all. My prayer is not yet answered."

I finished the story.

"O Padri Sahib, if I had only known the ending all these forty years, how much more quietly I should have waited in the darkness for the Shepherd. For forty years I had feared the lamb was lost."

I rose again.

"The end of the story has given me strength to have you go, for the Shepherd kept the lamb upon his shoulder. The lamb was not lost again, you say?"

"It was not lost again," I repeated.

We walked out to the road. He was a different man now—youth and sight seemed to have returned to him.

"Let me go ahead, Padri Sahib, and show you the way. There are many trees. Be careful lest you stumble. I would carry that which brought the Answer—I know not what to call it—if I knew where to take hold—"

"It is heavy, Bare Mian."

"But I am strong to-day, Padri Sahib. I have had bread, you know."

"It runs itself, Bare Mian, with just a touch now and then."

"With just a touch now and then? Then it is like our village, Padri Sahib. So might we run ourselves along the ways of God with just a touch now and then."

"Your village, Bare Mian? Does your village know anything of truth?"

"It knows the Lord's Prayer. For forty years the children have learned it from me. When you return, Padri Sahib, with the help now of the story, I shall have it ready for the water. And you need not be sparing of water, for our wells are deep. I shall hold the vessel—that will be my privilege—like this I will hold it."

He stopped and turned, laughing in his excitement, as some child in eager expectation of some great event.

"But what if you stumble, Bare Mian, and spill the water?"

"Then the ground will be baptized, and all will be Christian, Padri Sahib."

I bade him farewell, promising to send some one from my pitifully small body of native helpers, and to return myself some time within a year. With his forehead on his folded hands he stood till I was gone. As I rode off I heard him shout in a shrill, sharp voice to some toiler in a near-by field:

"Ram Lal! The lamb was found, Ram Lal! the lamb of the story was found!"

XII

WITH THE GODS IN MUTTRA

IT was the peculiar Persian pattern of her *chadar* that had first attracted my attention. Its unusual colors and the gracefulness of its folds over her head and shoulders had caught my eye as I stepped from the train at Muttra.

I had come for a day with my camera in that ancient stronghold of Hinduism. Long before the day was over I had used up all my plates. Who would not, in Muttra?

It was then, just inside the magnificent Harding gateway, in the midst of that bazaar of never-ending interest, that I caught sight again of the young Hindu woman with the pretty Persian pattern on her veil.

I was about to start for the mission house to rest and write awhile, but a new idea came to me. Why not follow this woman, as she went along through the crowded bazaar, and see what she would do? It was not an impulse springing from mere curiosity; there was a real desire for a more intimate knowledge of the people. I knew the language—I could understand all that I might hear.

My decision was quickly made, and I turned back and took up the trail. There was no danger of anyone knowing what I was doing, for the bazaar was thronged with people—almost like Fifth Avenue in New York at luncheon time. I did not feel as if I were intruding. I was ready, however, for an experience. It came—I never spent a more illuminating day.

Together let us follow the Hindu woman.

She stopped in a short time at a little box of a shop, measuring about five by eight feet, where were displayed all manner of boys' caps, made mostly of white muslin, embroidered with gold tinsel. She picked them over for a while, hesitated over one of the more elaborately embroidered ones, and finally bought it. She passed on, and holding it up extended on her outstretched fingers, exclaimed aloud to herself: "How fine it would look on his head!"

Just then all unnoticed a monkey ran along the edge of a veranda, jumped on the branch of a nim tree that overhung the narrow street, and, swinging down, snatched the cap from her hand. The next instant he was back on the top of an adjoining portico, where he sat and deliberately tore the little cap into bits, flinging them down into the street.

The woman had given a startled cry as the monkey grabbed the cap, and now she stood in the midst of the crowd that had stopped to watch the monkey. It was a matter of passing interest. Muttra is full of monkeys—"sacred monkeys," incarnations, as it were, of Hanuman, the great monkey-god. They are a pest in the city, breaking down cornices, loosening bricks and mortar on the parapets of houses, breaking window panes, destroying latticework, uprooting flowers and vegetables in the gardens, and in themselves a perfect nuisance. The shopkeepers suffer most at their mischievous, impudent hands, for the wares are always open to display on the stalls fronting the street. Up above, on the verandas, are the monkeys, ever alert, watching their chance to slide down a post or pillar and make off with a handful of grain, sweetmeats, or anything else fancied by the impudent creatures.

A Hindu can swear at a monkey, he can threaten it. He might dare to go so far as to hit one. He cannot go further to rid himself of one of these "gods"! The imagination does not go so far as to think of shooting one! His anger, kindled for the moment, will turn ultimately into philosophy.

"Remember Hanuman, the great god, my daughter," said a pious old merchant who had witnessed the affair of the cap, "and be content with the trifling loss."

The crowd moved on. The monkey had been making suitable grimaces during his work of destruction; and he sent his parting shot at me, as I leveled the camera at him! He would have had my scalp, had he dared!

As the woman moved on, I heard her mutter: "Is it a bad omen?"

I did not know *then* what she had in mind.

Almost immediately, however, she got a chance to counteract the apparently untoward event.

A Hindu faqir, tall, strong, and well fed, came down the street, leading an unusually small cow. The level of its back was not more than three feet from the ground. But the most striking thing about it was a queer deformity. High up on one side toward the front, there grew from the body two short misshapen legs. The hoofs were on them, dangling half way down to the ground.

The faqir had stopped just before the woman came up. He was talking to a small group of passers-by.

"Put your money right here," said he, indicating the spot where the extra legs took their start. "It will please Mahadeo, whose blessings will be showered on you. What a chance to do a meritorious thing in our great Muttra!"

The woman had heard his words.

"Will it bring good luck?" she asked, timidly, as she approached the faqir.

"Luck!" exclaimed the ash-smeared

rascal. "It will turn bad luck into good, or good luck into bad, just as I may please!" He had sized up his victim.

She deposited two copper coins on the "sacred spot," and the faqir said to her, "How much 'luck' can you get with two pice, O woman! Make that silver, and your chances are quadrupled!"

His countenance was grave. She hesitated a moment, then added to the copper coins a silver coin worth four times as much. The faqir muttered an unintelligible blessing, and started for his next dupe.

The woman moved on down the street.

She stopped shortly at the shop of a confectioner, whose wares—many of them coated with silver foil beaten by hand to an amazing thinness—were attractively displayed. She bought some *peras,* for which I knew Muttra was justly famous. I could have eaten the *peras* myself, but for the flies that swarmed in myriads from the open drain that ran reeking with filth right under the framework of a counter on which were piled the pyramids of sweets. That drain was appalling to an American, even though

"High up on one side there grew two short misshapen legs"

he had lived in India nearly his whole life!

The woman turned into an alley and went up the road that led along the river bank.

A little distance up this quaint street, under a scrubby pipal tree was a group of men and women. Coming up to them I saw an ascetic. He was seated amidst his four sacred fires, kept smoldering by means of the fuel cakes of *gobar* (cow-dung mixed with straw). I gathered from the conversation of several pilgrims in the group that he had been rather rudely awakened from sleep by the falling of a piece of a dead limb from the pipal tree. It had broken under the weight of a monkey, and fallen on one of his fires from which a live coal had been knocked over on to his leg. Apparently, he either did not accept or understand the explanation.

Idle curiosity caused the woman to push her way to the inner edge of the circle.

The faqir caught sight of her and exclaimed, "May the curse of the gods be upon thee!"

The woman stood as if paralyzed, while the faqir continued, apparently to the onlookers: "What does she in Muttra anyway? Always it is a woman that is at the bottom of a man's troubles!"

He had relieved himself by this outburst, and turned to replenish the fires of his self-torture; but the poor woman was trembling with fear under the sudden and so unexpected imprecation of the "holy one."

She fell on her knees at his feet.

"O, Maharaj," she wailed, "pardon the fault of thy slave! Truly, I did not understand. I own my guilt—I should not have dared to interrupt thy holy meditations by idly thrusting myself before thee. We are so slow to learn the ways of the holy!"

She had no slightest idea of any injustice done to herself. She did not know what had caused the curse to descend upon her. She was just a woman—she should not have dared to approach the sacred person of the devoted faqir in such a spirit of reprehensible curiosity. But the curse must be undone!

She prostrated herself at the feet of the ash-smeared, high and mighty, stern and offended "holy one." He affected not to see her. She crawled nearer, took hold of his feet around the ankles and kissed them repeatedly.

"Pardon—forgiveness—mercy, O holy Sadhu!" she moaned. "Terrible is the weight of thy most righteous curse. I am only a woman—I wist not what I did—I cannot bear the awful burden of thy just but fearful anathema!"

He drew back his feet with impatience, and left her kissing the ground in her grief and terror. The poor woman was almost distracted. If there was any sympathy among the numerous onlookers, fear of the enraged faqir kept it back. True, he was no genuine *Sadhu* who would thus be offended by any untoward event. Even if the accident were the result of malice, the very profession of a *Sadhu* should have enabled him to bear with either hurt or insult. This fellow was a rogue, a charlatan; but even so, there was no one minded to run the risk of his curse. Who knew but that he had acquired special merit from the gods by self-torture, and could blast the fairest prospects of anyone now daring to interfere. After all, why *had* the woman crowded to the front in that bold fashion? Was the curse not deserved? Had she not brought it upon herself?

My American spirit could not endure the scene. I was touched by the woman's genuine terror, and incensed at the faqir's cruel attempt to "save his face," I stepped up before him, and said in Hindustani:

"O, Sadhuji, the woman is not at fault—we all are witness here. Her petition is just. Unsay the curse!"

I had drawn his fire. He fastened his

eyes upon me, and gave an unusually loud cough, as if seeking to bring himself fully to alertness.

"So it is you, the white-faced foreigner, who is at the bottom of it all!" he exclaimed, and then, catching sight of my camera, added, "with your infernal new-fangled machine, that will yet be the undoing of all that is sacred in our great Hindustan!"

He looked at me steadily, with a determined penetration, and I realized that he sought to intimidate me by his stare. It was a duel! I stared back unflinchingly. He was trying to hypnotize me by his look. The faqirs all deal with the occult and mystical. I set my jaws with grim determination, and looked down into the depths of his eyes. Neither of us stirred. The crowd became silent, wondering what would come next. It came from the Sadhu—I was determined that it should.

"I transfer the curse to you!" he exclaimed. This brought the woman to a sitting posture.

"And I," said I, deliberately and with all the solemnity I could muster, "can bear your curse unmoved. Its weight is like the feather's on the strong wing of the eagle. It gives added strength to battle with the elements!"

I awaited the effect of these words and soon saw a look of apprehension steal into his face. I knew he was unequal to the situation, and so I added, with a tone of magnanimity:

"And I will show you the heart of a *true* Sadhu, one who has given up all for the sake of your own fair Hindustan. I give you my blessing in return for your curse. May the peace that the world can neither give nor take away come into your life. May the light that shines more fair and bright than Indra's beams on the snow-white breast of Himachal enlighten your dark path. May the power that comes from the anointing of the Almighty God be upon you, and turn your weakness into strength."

The man felt the melting heat of the coals of fire thus heaped on his head. My words had doubtless caused to leap up within him an admiration for one who could return a blessing for a curse—and a blessing of such magnitude, couched in terms to him so new! He turned to the crowd and said:

"The gods themselves could not curse such a one! The Sahib is a true Sadhu. The Sadhu reveres the Sadhu."

He had saved his face! He replenished his fires with some more fuel cakes and, turning toward the river, plunged in meditation.

The incident was closed. The crowd moved on, their faith in *Sadhus* unshaken! I took up the trail of the Persian pattern. The woman had continued along the river road.

"What is the tower?" I heard her asking of a group of Bengali widows, on a pilgrimage to Muttra, eight hundred miles from home.

"That," replied one of the widows, as she turned wistful eyes on the tower of brown sandstone, "is the Sati tower, erected in lasting remembrance of the good women of bygone days who here in Muttra mounted the funeral pyres of their husbands and ended noble lives by glorious deaths!"

"The Sarcar [government] is kind in its

thought in passing a law against Sati," said another of the widows, "but it would be easier to die once for all than to know the living death that is ours!"

"You speak foolishly," replied a third. "You burn your hand the way I accidentally did not long ago, and then let us see how ready you are for the flames of the Sati!"

"I dread such pain too," said the woman I was following, "but how many problems it would solve for some!"

I took it she was depressed after her experience with the *sadhu*. Her clothes and jewelry showed she was not a widow, but I thought she felt the burden of being *just a woman.* It is a burden prepared by Hindu men and Hindu law for all Hindu womankind. The time draws near when the burden is to be lifted.

She moved on up the street. In an angle formed by a little temple and an adjoining shop lay a faqir on a bed of spikes. At the foot of the wooden platform that bore the iron spikes was a place for the offerings of passers-by. A number of copper and a few silver coins were in evidence. To these she added two pice, and moved on without a word.

"How long have you been on this bed of spikes?" I asked the faqir, a man with a white beard, between fifty and sixty years old. He deigned no reply.

"The holy one is meditating, Sahib," said his young disciple, barely twenty years of age, covered with ashes, seated beside his *guru* (master). "I have heard him tell others," he continued, "that he has spent thirty years thus."

No one thought it strange. Beds of spikes

are as common in India as beds of roses in America!

I would have continued the conversation, but my Persian pattern was almost out of sight in the crowd ahead.

The afternoon had now drawn to a close—the hour of evening worship had come. The temple courts were thronged, the temple bells were ringing. The pilgrims filled the streets, the little shops were busy selling doles of rice, oil, *ghee,* powdered paint, flowers, and the many small necessities of the devotees who seemed eager to carry out to the letter the instructions of the priests.

The woman seemed tired, and seated herself on the stone steps that lead down to the river from this street along the bank of the stream. It gave me another opportunity to watch the crowd of worshipers.

Quite close to us I noticed a group of five—ignorant, village folk—going through the absurd minutia of the formula of prayers for the souls of their deceased loved ones. With what a simple and eager faith they followed the strange directions of the priest! They thought of the benefit to the spirits of the departed, he only of the fees! How cold and callous he had become!

Many pilgrims who had come too late in the day to bathe earlier in the sacred stream were now going through the forms of ceremonial purification. There is a woman taking the three sacred dips in one breath. Yonder is a man pouring out water as a libation to the gods. Here is a group, waist deep in the water, muttering prayers under the guidance of a priest.

Men selling garlands of marigolds and jasmine are going to and fro among the bathers and worshipers offering their fragrant wares for sale. The gods always love flowers! Look at yonder stone image of the elephant-headed Ganesh, loaded with wreaths of the yellow *gendas* and white *chambelis*. See, the attendant at the shrine is putting another flowery necklace over the willing head of the god of wisdom. He is doing it for the youth who stands close by with the palms of his hands joined in supplication. He is doubtless a student in some school. The time of the annual examination is drawing nigh, and he is anxious to have the support of the god of wisdom in his uncertain scholastic effort. Yes, the priest will go through some special prayers, if the proper offerings are made! 'Tis wondrous indeed how offerings to the gods fit in with the needs of those who minister at their shrines!

The fat and jolly *halwai* (confectioner) who passes is devoted to Lakhshmi, the goddess of wealth. Why dote on the god of wisdom when the gods have already bestowed on you sense enough to acquire bags full of rupees, and wisdom enough to enjoy the fine flour, *ghee* and sweets that the skill of the gods themselves have enabled you to combine in such delicious fashion! 'Tis all the same, whether one follows the solemn Ganesh, the blood-thirsty Kali, or the handsome Sri Krishna, who in the most pleasing form of all took incarnation here in Muttra, making the city world renowned by his knavish tricks as a boy and his fondness for the pretty *gopis* (shepherdesses) when grown up. True, the priests, the modern devotees of Krishna in his own native city, did not have the *gopis,* but was there any lack of "daughters of the gods" in the temple cloisters! *Halwai* and priest met and passed: each understood the other.

The woman was interested in watching the turtles. They swarm in the river, espe-

cially along this bank with its temples and worshipers. The turtle is sacred too, and the pilgrims feed them. It is one of the best known direct methods of feeding the gods! After a while the woman got up, walked across the street to a little temporary shop, tucked in between two shrines, and bought a few coppers' worth of popped rice—the same thing that forms one of our "new" breakfast foods in America, eaten in India by men, monkeys, and turtles before America was on the map of the world. She returned to the river and flung handfuls of the white flakes into the water along the steps. In an instant they were snapped down by the waiting turtles. I thought of "Cast thy bread upon the waters," but I knew there could be no "finding" of this bread again!

She mounted the steps and proceeded up the river road. Where an alley entered it on the left from the city, a faqir had found room enough to spread out a bit of blanket, on one end of which stood a carved wooden image of Krishna. His body was painted the rich blue to which the god is partial, and he was shown playing the flute, in his usual attitude, standing on one foot. The man in charge of the idol held aloft with his left hand a big gong which he pounded vigorously with a mallet in his right hand. Meantime, he eloquently invited the noble-minded passers-by to deposit their offerings to Sri Krishna on the other end of the

"We had reached the great temple that . . . opens out . . . on to the river"

blanket. His efforts had not been in vain, for there was a sprinkling of coins on the spot of advantage. To this store the woman added a few coppers. She seemed to leave nothing undone that a pious Hindu woman could do. In everything she had done thus far I had noted an earnestness and sincerity that compelled my admiration.

By this time we had reached the great temple that fronts the main street of the city on one side, and on the other opens out with a spacious paved court on to the river. Here every evening at dusk is celebrated the now rare service of the *Arthi*, the fire-worship. I had seen it once before, and wondered if the woman would stay for it.

The sun was down now, and the short Indian twilight would soon pass into darkness. Preparations for the *Arthi* were under way, but there was time for the beautiful ceremony of sending little lighted floats down the river.

The woman went to a man seated in a sort of balcony to one side of the court of the temple, and from him she purchased three things. One was a queer little raft, about nine by six inches, made of pieces of coarse, stiff straw. This cost one pice (half a cent). Then she purchased three saucer-like clay dishes for another pice, and for two pice got enough crude mustard oil to fill the dishes. A cotton dip for each dish came free with the oil. With these things in her hands she asked for the services of one of the priests, and together they went down the steps to the river's edge. The dishes were put on the little raft, and the wicks were lighted from the sacred fire within the temple. Mystic words of incantation were murmured, and then the frail craft was launched and gently pushed out into the current. It was bearing some message to the unseen world, and however indifferent the priest or the general company of on-lookers, there was one that watched with emotion as the tiny raft made its precarious way down the stream. The woman stood, peering into the dusk, her whole thought on the life of her tiny raft.

Many other worshipers were setting adrift similar little lights, and the river afforded a beautiful sight. Altogether, I thought I had never watched any scene of Hindu worship that struck me as being so quaint and attractive. Far down the stream the flickering lights could be seen. A barge that was being forced up the river by means of long poles pushed against the bottom of the stream, made straight for a squadron of the little rafts among which was the one that the woman was watching. The boat bumped into some of the rafts and sank them. Hers escaped, and she gave an exclamation of relief. She was like a child in her solicitude for it. But she was to be disappointed, for the wavelets started by the barge struck the little messenger of light, and the next instant its tiny flame disappeared.

The incident was a most ordinary one—but not for her. This was her first visit to Muttra, evidently, and she took everything very seriously. Also she was young and inexperienced. The sinking of her "light ship" troubled her, and again she spoke aloud to herself: "I wonder—is it a bad omen?"

The crowd was beginning to surge in for

the *Arthi* worship. The woman, to escape the throng, had seated herself at the end of an outer balcony of the temple court that extended on each side toward the river. I had had previous experience of the jostling of the multitude at the hour of the *Arthi,* and so I hailed a bargeman who was loitering near with the hope of being hired to take a load of passengers up or down stream, or possibly across to the villages on the other bank. I was not intending to leave yet—the barge would give me the best opportunity of seeing the *Arthi.*

My interest in the woman had greatly increased because of what I had seen her go through during the afternoon. I wondered now if she would share in the fire worship.

The scene before me was this: A large temple in the background, with extensions to the right and left, forming a kind of courtyard on the river front. The inclosed space was paved with stones, the outer edge descending with a flight of steps to the river's edge. In the middle of the court, but on the side nearest the water, was a stone table of the ordinary height, about four by six feet. From the corners of this, but allowing some space between, rose six carved stone pillars, on whose tops rested heavy stone beams. From these were suspended several bells of various size.

When the time of the celebration of the *Arthi* had arrived, three priests appeared from the temple and began ringing the bells. The ringing was continuous, unlike any temple bells I had heard during the day. The sounds jarred, and there was an insistency about the ringing that was likely to get on one's nerves. With the continual appeal of the bells, the crowd surged in. The river road, along which we had come, emptied directly into the temple courtyard.

I bade the bargeman push up close to the stone steps so that I might get a better view. The people on the steps were coming and going, some late comers even now performing their little religious ceremonies. But it was not all religion with those at the water's edge. Some washed their feet, some rinsed out travel-stained garments, some "brushed" their teeth, using their fingers and liberal quantities of powdered charcoal.

Some filled their *lotas* with the sacred water, and others drank it. In the midst of it all the slimy turtles kept moving around, snapping at bits of food floating on the surface. It was a strange sight! Where, but in India, could one find its like?

Meantime the temple bells kept up their clangor. The waiting multitudes crowded the courts and filled the balconies. Then the bells ceased, and through the crowd came a priest, bearing aloft a flaming metallic candlestick, with several circular platforms, one rising above another. On the outer edge of each of these were several little receptacles for oil, in which were burning cotton wicks. He came to the stone table, which he mounted and, facing the river, went through a series of fantastic wavings. It was a weird scene—the deepening shadows upon the temple in the background, the strange, expectant figures that waited behind the priest, the dark current of the river lapping the sides of my barge.

When the ceremony of waving and incantations was over, the priest placed the flaming candlestick on the table, while he and two other priests took their stand beside the table.

"Come forward now, and get the touch of the sacred fire," exclaimed one of the priests, "but bring your offerings with you," he added, "and place them on the table."

The crowd surged forward. Their enthusiasm was refreshing, and I gave myself up to a study of the scene. Each one, on approaching the table, dropped some offering of money at the base of the candlestick, and then passed a hand rapidly through the flames. The devotee then touched his forehead with his hand. This was done three times by each one—unless the crowd pushed the worshiper past the fire before all three touches could be secured. In that case one touch would suffice. This became increasingly the case as the multitude behind became the more eager to reach the fire.

I noticed the faces of the people. There were pilgrims, men and women, who had journeyed far on foot to spend a few days among the far-famed shrines and temples of Muttra. Here came a group of hard-headed farmers, men for whom this was one of the crowning experiences of life, for which they had planned and saved for many years. There were many widows among the crowd, poor, broken creatures, with their coarse garments and short-clipped hair. What tales of misery, cruelty, and degradation could those uncomplaining lips tell if they would speak!

I looked at the priests. The face of one, the leader, was keen and strong, but hard, unrelenting. Another looked cunning, but weakly sensual. The third showed pure animal.

The crowd did not move along fast enough to suit the chief of the priests: the flames of the *Arthi* would die down before all the devotees had had an opportunity to reach the table! The offerings would be reduced. A company of slow village folk who took an unduly long time in getting the touch of the sacred fire, yet deposited but little money—all copper—tried his patience beyond endurance. Repeatedly had he and his fellow priests urged the crowds to increase their offerings and accelerate their steps. It would require more than exhortations! I saw him reach down under the table and take a long piece of cloth, probably a turban not then in use. This he tied at one end into several large knots, and began to use it in savage style, laying it across the backs and shoulders of those who happened to offend him.

"Move on, you wretch!" he shouted at a young villager who, apparently overpowered by his emotions as he took the touch of the sacred fire upon him, forgot to heed the injunctions for speed. The knotted *pugri* descending on his shoulders brought him quickly to a realization that his feet were still upon the earth! Strangely enough, he did not realize that the priests looked on the people almost as so many cattle!

It was at this time that my eyes wandered over the crowd, and I caught sight of the woman in the Persian pattern. She was back on the outer edge of the throng, making her way down toward the table. She came slowly, but as eager to reach the fire as any. When she came nearer I noticed a woman next to her who was carrying a baby.

The mother was quite short in stature, and apparently frail. The two were talking together. As they finally neared the table, I saw the mother hand the child to the other woman.

By this time the fires were burning low, and the throng pressed closer than ever to get the undoubted benefit of a touch of the sacred flame. There was no time now for the desired three touches. The two women whom I was watching were rudely jostled. The mother made a dart with her hand at the fire and barely reached it. The other was stronger and more determined. She passed her hand through the fire and touched her forehead, but before she was beyond reach she managed another coveted touch. This time she carried her hand to the baby and touched his forehead.

It was a beautiful thing. The whole scene had deeply impressed me, and made me realize anew the passionate yearning of the ordinary man or woman of India for all that is bound up with existence in the life beyond. What mighty things are in store for India when her sons and daughters have found the true Light, have felt the touch of the real Fire from on high!

The tender thoughtfulness of the woman for the little child had deeply touched me. I admired her more than ever. On the outer edge of the crowd she placed the baby in its mother's arms, and the latter moved on. The woman waited. The throng was melting away. The flames of the *Arthi* had died down. I stepped from the barge on to the flight of steps, and followed the priests up toward the temple. It was now almost dark, and only a few worshipers remained.

The woman addressed one of the priests.

"Maharaj," she said, "I am a woman in distress and need thy help."

"In distress!" he exclaimed. "Hast thou not joined, then, in the *Arthi* worship?"

"Yes, but the touch of the fire does not heal the sorrow of my heart. Most holy one," she said, joining the palms of her hands together in supplication, "I am a childless wife. Is there help from the gods for me?"

Then I understood her remark about the

boy's cap she had bought. Then I recalled her apprehension lest there should be bad luck in any of the happenings of the day. I remembered her readiness to do everything she could to win the favor of the devotees and their gods. She perhaps was imagining she carried her own child in her arms at the *Arthi* worship!

"Hast thou proved thy earnestness to the gods?" he asked. "Hast backed up thy petitions with gifts?" He was thinking of the fees that might be forthcoming.

"I have taken long and weary pilgrimages. I went once to Puri, and paid much to gaze upon the lotus-face of Jagannath. I visited the shrines at Adjudhiya to win the favor of Ram, who showed such deep love for his faithful Sita. The answer of the gods has been only silence."

Another of the priests spoke up.

"Hast thou invoked the favor of our Lord Krishna of Muttra?"

"I came but this day," she replied. "I seek those who can help me to the favor of the adored Sri Krishna."

The second man evidently thought of her

money. His glance was on the silver anklets, the costly bracelets, and the silver ornaments that decked her neck and ears. Many such costly ornaments had found their way to his hand via the gods!

"Make sure thy case here with Lord Krishna, but withhold not the silver and the gold that so delight his heart. He hears the better when the tinkle of coins and jewelry is in his ears."

The third priest took up the conversation. He it was whom I have called "all animal"!

"Thou art fair of form and face, and art young besides," said he. "The gods themselves are not indifferent to such things in their petitioners! Sri Krishna loved to look upon the beauty of the *gopis*. Methinks he had an eye for youthful comeliness if any ever had! Thy plea is surer far, since thou art favored by the gods with beauty. Take courage fresh, and approach in hope the sacred precincts."

He turned to the other priests.

"Say ye not, O reverend companions, that now the hour has struck for the prayers of all her past to be answered, here at last?"

"Ay," replied the first, who bore the still warm *Arthi* candlestick, "she nears at length the haven of her desires."

The other continued his theme.

"The ways of the gods are known best to those who live most near them. We dwell within the shadows of these temples, we can assure thee. Come now with us. Spend but a night within the holy precincts of these cloisters, and thy petition shall be granted, or—the gods themselves are impotent!"

They started toward the entrance to the temple inclosure. She hesitated, and then followed them. I do not think she understood the import of the words of the third priest.

I understood!

I stood where I had been, in the shadow of one of the balconies, as I had listened to the conversation with the priests. Would she enter that door, with the priests, into the inner inclosure of the temple?

As they neared the entrance, I noticed the forms of several women pass before a light within the temple. They were young women—they were the "devadasis," the *daughters of the gods.*

The woman hesitated at the door. She began to understand! An instant later she turned suddenly away, and made her way rapidly along the temple inclosure. She entered an alley that led back into the main thoroughfare, and was gone.

I turned, with a sigh of relief, toward the river. Out in the current a tiny raft of straw, bearing a single light, went floating down the stream. It had come thus far safely on its uncertain way.

I thought of the woman. It was a good omen! The abyss had not yet swallowed her. But I knew she was on a treacherous way—the darkness surrounded her.

. . . .

Five years passed. I was back again in Muttra, attending a convention at the Mission Training School for Christian women. European, Indian, and Anglo-Indian young women were receiving a practical training for Christian service.

Among the candidates was a new arrival —an Indian woman with a little child. Her story was on the lips of all. She had been a pilgrim. Her husband had died and she had wandered far from shrine to shrine, carrying her child with her. She sought enlightenment—peace for a distracted spirit.

She came a few weeks since on a pilgrimage to Muttra—had been there before. In the darkness of that heathen stronghold the light suddenly shone in on her. She heard a man preach of a Saviour. It was what she sought. She listened, and heard for the first time the story of the love of Jesus. Her hungry heart cried out for him. She forgot Krishna, and Ram, and Jagannath. She had found Christ! She spoke to the preacher, and he brought her to the missionaries at the Training School. Now she was learning to read. Some day—soon, she hoped—she could herself carry the message, out into the darkness from which she had come.

Later in the day I saw her, studying with a group under the shade of a spreading *nim* tree. Something in her face made me think of the Hindu woman with the Persian pattern, whom I had followed through the crowded streets of Muttra a few years ago. It was a passing fancy. It could not be she—this woman was considerably older.

Just then her child—a girl of three—came running toward her from behind the tree. She was draped in a little chadar with a *Persian pattern!* Material and figures were identical with the one so well remembered.

I looked at the mother, as she lifted her smiling face to her winsome little daughter. The love-light had taken away ten years from her looks. I recognized the woman with the Persian pattern!

I had left her in the darkness. I found her in the light!